SCHOOL IS DEAD

EVERETT REIMER has studied the questions of educational reform for many years through various offices and agencies. His experience in working on the Committee of Human Resources in Puerto Rico coupled with extensive work with Ivan Illich at the CIDOC center in Cuernavaca, Mexico, led to some of the ideas proposed in SCHOOL IS DEAD. In recent years, Mr. Reimer has led CIDOC's yearly seminars on "Alternatives in Education." He presently teaches at the University of Puerto Rico.

SCHOOL IS DEAD:
Alternatives in Education

EVERETT REIMER

ANCHOR BOOKS
DOUBLEDAY & COMPANY, INC.
GARDEN CITY, NEW YORK
1972

SCHOOL IS DEAD: ALTERNATIVES IN EDUCATION
was published in a hardcover edition by
Doubleday & Company, Inc. in 1971.
Anchor Books Edition: 1972
Excerpts from *The New Industrial State,* by John
Kenneth Galbraith. Copyright © 1967 by John
Kenneth Galbraith. Reprinted by permission of
Houghton Mifflin Company.

My grandmother wanted me to have an education,
so she kept me out of school.

Margaret Mead

CONTENTS

FOREWORD

This book is the result of a conversation with Ivan Illich that has continued for fifteen years. We have talked of many things, but increasingly about education and school and, eventually, about alternatives to schools.

Illich and I met in Puerto Rico, where I had come in 1954 as secretary of the Committee on Human Resources of the commonwealth government, charged with assessing the manpower needs of the island and recommending an educational program to meet them. Puerto Rico was then in the course of rapid industrialization, and my calculations showed that dropout rates would have to decline throughout the school system if the estimated manpower needs of the economy were to be met. Everything was done to reduce these rates and they actually declined for a while, but it soon became apparent that the decline was at the expense of grade standards and, therefore, meaningless.

Illich came to Puerto Rico in 1956, at the request of the late Cardinal Spellman, to organize a training program for New York priests from parishes overrun by Puerto Rican migrants. We soon found common interests and many parallels in the problems of church and school. In 1960 Illich left Puerto Rico for Mexico,[1] and shortly afterward I joined the Alliance for Progress. We began to study the problems of Latin American education at about the same time, and these turned out to be similar to the problems of Puerto Rico but on a vastly larger scale. It was soon clear to both of us that the countries of Latin America could not, for many years, afford schools for all their children. At the same time, education seemed to be the basic need of these countries, not only to us but also to their political parties and leaders. In 1968 we began a systematic study of this dilemma and of possible ways out of it.

Our analysis of schools was soon extended to other institutions and to the structure of the society schools serve. At first we felt that school was a lagging institution in an increasingly efficient technological society. We later came to see schools as providing indispensable support for a technological society that is itself not viable. The simplest way to expose the contradictions of this society is to point out that it promises unlimited progress to unlimited numbers of people. The absurdity of this claim is conceded by the recognition of the need for birth control, but birth control itself turns out to depend on progress. Women have fewer children if they have been to school for at least four years, but by the time children can be kept in school long enough for this to have a significant impact on birth rates, the population of the world will have increased threefold. And this is using conservative projections. If modern medical techniques were made generally available, the rate of population increase would double or triple.[2] We retain breathing space only by letting poor babies die at ten times the rate of privileged babies.

During the past decade the actual rate at which living standards have improved among the underprivileged peoples of the world is scarcely greater than the rate of population growth. On a per-capita basis, individuals have benefited marginally, if at all.

Part of the problem lies in the inefficiency of modern institutions, including schools. The greater part lies in the open-ended nature of the promise of progress. As the world is now organized, the standard of living in India can rise consistently only if the standard of living in the United States also rises. Because of its effects on the demand for Indian exports and upon the supply of American capital abroad, stagnation of the American economy tends to depress the economic growth of

India. Yet, a normal rise in the United States average income is twice the total income of the average Indian. Raising world consumption standards to U.S. levels would multiply the combustion of fossil fuels by fifty times, the use of iron a hundred times, the use of other metals over two hundred times. By the time these levels were reached, consumption levels in the United States would again have tripled and the population of the world would also have tripled. Such projections lead to results as absurd as the premises from which they start. There can be no open-ended progress. Yet this is what modern institutions promise. This is the promise of science and technology unrestrained by reason. This is the promise that has promoted the growth of schools and other modern institutions and that they in turn propagate. Schools produce the subjects of a world in which technology is king.

The contradictions of such a world are becoming apparent. They are best illustrated in the school and best corrected by freeing education from the school so that people may learn the truth about the society in which they live.

In the course of this analysis, an interpretation of human history has developed that, although sketchy and incomplete, must be shared with the reader. When techniques, institutions, and ideologies were primitive, men lived in relative equality and freedom, because there were no adequate means of domination. As techniques, institutions, and ideologies developed, they were used to establish and maintain relations of domination and privilege. From that time on, the societies that succeeded in dominating others, and thus world history, were also characterized by interclass and interpersonal domination in tension with efforts to establish equality. As techniques increased in efficiency and ideologies in scope, they repeatedly threatened to upset the privilege structure of society. Institutions were used to counter these threats by controlling the use of the techniques and by perverting the ideologies. When revolutionary breakthroughs occurred, institutions were re-established on a broader base, extending privilege to more people, but always at the same time maintaining the structure of privilege. This view does not necessarily lead to a Jeffersonian suspicion of institutions as such. Despite the historical record, the possibility of democratic institutions remains—if men determine to use institutions for democratic purposes.

I would like to be able to say that the previous paragraph contains the last oversimplification in this book. Regrettably, I cannot. I have tried to qualify my assertions, to provide evidence for them, to give supporting references, and to justify my value judgments, but I do not expect to satisfy the norms of academic scholarship. To do that I would have to write not this book now but a completely different book twenty years from now. I chose to write this book now because I would like to live to see it become a self-fulfilling prophecy. Twenty years from now I might not be alive.

My view of history does not result in an unbiased appraisal of schools nor of the society to which schools belong but rather in an indictment of both. Schools are admittedly treated in stereotype rather than in terms of concrete human behavior. Schools are simply too big to treat concretely. Alternatives to school, as opposed to mere reform, require going beyond the experience of individuals to an analysis of the essential characteristics of schools. Nevertheless, in an abstract treatment people will not quite recognize themselves as students, teachers, or parents, or in other concrete roles related to schools. A few may feel themselves cast as the villains in a conspiracy of injustice. But this would be a misreading of the book.

There are unjust men in the world and it is an unjust world, but it is not the unjust men, as such, who make it so. It is an unjust world largely because it is composed of faulty institutions. These institutions, in turn, are merely the collective habits of individuals, but individuals can have bad habits without being bad people. In general, people are unconscious of their habits, particularly their institutional habits. One thesis of this book is that people can become aware of their bad habits and can change them. The world would then be a better world, made up of still-imperfect people. There are, of course, some people who know that they have bad habits but do not want to change them. There are others who are afraid to examine their habits for fear that their consciences would then be troubled. This is the worst that can be said of most people. It is enough, however, to explain how the world can be worse than the people who live in it.

The realities of school are both better and worse than they are here described. Others have made more of an attempt at concrete portrayal, and their work is an indispensable supplement to the present analysis. Tom Brown, Charlie Brown, Miss Peach, and the children and teachers from George Dennison's[3] and Jonathan Kozol's[4] accounts are a few examples of the reality of school. A model for general description and analysis of institutional behavior is to be found in Floyd Allport's book by that name.[5]

This book owes far more debts than I can remember, let alone acknowledge. Several, however, I cannot forget. Except for the insistence of Ralph Bohrson it might never have been written. The Ford Foundation travel and study grant that he administered allowed me to spend time writing it that might otherwise have been spent on other work. Cooperation from CIDOC, which has permitted me to work intensively with Illich and to publish earlier drafts and discuss them with students and associates, has been even more vital. Many educators, economists, administrators, and political leaders from Latin America, the United States, and Europe have by this time participated in the analysis that Illich and I have conducted. Most of them are referred to in the text and in the appended notes. I want especially to recognize the invaluable editorial assistance of Jordan Bishop, George Dennison, John Holt, Monica Raymond, Joan Remple, Michael Samlowski, Dennis Sullivan, and of many students at CIDOC with whom I have discussed earlier drafts. Not least is the debt I owe my wife and sons and daughters for years of critical conversation about education and the rest of life. None of my collaborators is directly responsible for anything in the book. Even Illich may disagree with parts of it. By the time it is published it is quite likely that I will too.

SCHOOL IS DEAD

1. THE CASE AGAINST SCHOOLS

"If sharks were people," his landlady's little daughter asked Mr. K, "would they be nicer to the little fish?" "Of course," he said, "if sharks were people, they would have strong boxes built in the sea for little fish. There they would put in all sorts of food, plants and little animals, too. They would see to it that the boxes always had fresh water, and they would take absolutely every sort of sanitary measure. When, for example, a little fish would injure his fin, it would be immediately bandaged so that he would not die on the sharks before his time had come. In order that the little fish would never be sad, there would be big water parties from time to time; for happy fish taste better than sad ones. Of course, there would be schools in the big boxes as well. There the little fish would learn how to swim into the mouths of the sharks. They would need, for example, geography so that they could find the sharks, lazing around somewhere. The main subject would naturally be the moral education of the little fish. They would be taught that the grandest, most beautiful thing is for a little fish to offer himself happily, and that they must all believe in the sharks, above all when they say that they will provide for a beautiful future. One would let the little fish know that this future is only assured when they learn obedience. They must shy away from all lowly, materialistic and Marxist inclinations, and inform the sharks immediately if any one of them betrayed such tendencies. . . . If sharks were people, there would of course be art as well. There would be beautiful pictures of sharks' teeth, all in magnificent colors, of their mouths and throats as pure playgrounds where one can tumble and play. The theaters on the bottom of the sea would offer plays showing heroic little fish swimming enthusiastically down the throats of the sharks, and the music would be so beautiful that its sounds would lead the little fish dreamily to the chapels and, filled with the most pleasant thoughts, they would stream down the sharks' throats. There would certainly be religion. . . .

It would teach that true life really begins in the sharks' bellies. And if sharks were people, the little fish would stop being, as they are now, equals. Some would be given offices and be put over the others. Those a little bigger would even be allowed to eat the smaller ones. That would only be delightful for the sharks, for then they would more often have bigger crumbs to gobble up. And the most important of the little fish, those with offices, would look to the ordering of the little fish. And they would become teachers, officers, box-building engineers, etc. In short, there could only be culture in the sea if the sharks were people."

Bertolt Brecht, Kalendergeschichten

Most of the children of the world are not in school. Most of those who enter drop out after a very few years. Most of those who succeed in school still become dropouts at a higher level. UNESCO data show that only in a small minority of nations do even half the children complete the first six grades.[1] No child, however, fails to learn from school. Those who never get in, learn that the good things of life are not for them. Those who drop out early, learn that they do not deserve the good things of life. The later dropouts learn that the system can be beat, but not by them. All of them learn that school is the path to secular salvation, and resolve that their children shall climb higher on the ladder than they did.[2]

For most members of the present generation this hope, that their children will benefit more from school than they, is doomed to disappointment. Schools are too expensive for this hope to be realized. For many, it may appear to be realized, but the appearance will be a delusion fostered by inflationary debasement of the academic currency. More college and high school degrees will be granted, but they will mean less, both in terms of amount and kind of learning and in terms of job qualification and real income.

In all countries, school costs are rising faster than enrollments and faster than national income. While the school's share of national income can afford to grow slowly as this income increases, it cannot continue to grow at present rates. In Puerto Rico, for example, the national income was ten times greater in 1965 than in 1940. School enrollment more than doubled during this period, while school costs multiplied twenty-five times.[3] Yet, even in 1965, less than half of all Puerto Rican students finished nine years of school,[4] and the proportion who reached the higher grades without learning to read was higher than it had been twenty-five years earlier. Puerto Rico is atypical in its absolute rates of growth, but not in the vital relationships among them. Monographs on the cost of schooling in African and Asian countries, sponsored by the International Institute for Educational Planning, paint a similar picture, as do studies in Britain and most of the countries of western Europe.[5,6] Recent studies in the United States suggest that it would cost eighty billion additional dollars to meet educators' estimates of what is needed to provide adequate schooling.[7] Even the settlement of the war in Indochina would provide only a small fraction of this amount.

The conclusion is inescapable: No country in the world can afford the education its people want in the form of schools. Except for a few rich nations and some not yet exposed to the development virus, no country in the world can afford the schools its people are now demanding from their political leaders. Continued attempts to supply the demand for college study in the United States will condemn the black and rural minorities to an indefinite wait for an adequate education. In India, Nigeria, and Brazil the majority must, for generations, be denied all but marginal educational resources if a tiny minority is to enjoy the luxury of schooling that would still be regarded as pitifully inadequate by United States standards.

School is the world's largest enterprise; larger than agriculture, industry, or warfare. School's rivals for the educational dollar are demonstrably small by comparison. The mass media are the most prominent, the easiest to define, and the smallest. Large as the press and television are, along with movies, radio, and all other forms of publishing, broadcasting, and public entertainment, they account for less than half the time and money involved in schooling. This might not be true for the United States in terms of man-hours of exposure, but the rural masses of the rest of the world, as yet largely untouched by mass media, have all begun to send their children to school. On-the-job training, while harder to estimate, may be a little closer but still a losing rival to schools. There are a few more people at work throughout the world than in school, but not many more.[8] Not enough more to offset the smaller proportion of their work time devoted to learning.[9]

There are still people who believe that we could finance

the education we need by means of schooling, if only we were willing to give it priority, but this belief ignores the dynamics of schooling. No sooner is universal high school attendance approached than the competition shifts to colleges, at higher costs. There is already agitation for degrees above the Ph.D. on the grounds that the doctorate has become common and degraded. There can be no end to schooling in a world that puts no limits on consumption—where degrees determine people's position at the trough.

Schools are an almost perfectly regressive form of taxation, paid for by the poor to benefit the rich. Schools are supported, largely, by general taxes that ultimately fall more upon the poor than their direct incidence suggests. Property taxes, for example, are paid by those who occupy dwellings rather than by those who own them, excise taxes by consumers rather than producers. Meanwhile, the benefits of even public expenditures for schooling are distributed in direct proportion to present economic privilege.

The children of the poorest tenth of the United States population attend school for an average of less than five years. The schools they attend, at this grade level, spend no more than five hundred dollars per pupil per year. These children cost the public, in schooling, less than twenty-five hundred dollars each over a lifetime. The children of the richest tenth of the population finish college and a year of graduate school, which costs about thirty-five thousand dollars. Assuming that one third of this is private expenditure, the richest tenth still get ten times as much of public funds for education as the poorest tenth.[10]

Schools make it impossible to equalize educational opportunity, even in terms of the allocation of public resources. Unless they abandon scholastic standards altogether, they can never keep poor children in school as long as rich ones, and unless they reverse the cost ratios that have always characterized schooling, they will always spend more at higher than at lower levels. Even compensating programs specifically designed to help poor children cannot achieve their purpose within the present structure of the school. Of three billion dollars earmarked by the federal government of the United States for supplementary services to poor children, less than a third was actually spent on eligible children; these children showed no measurable improvement, while the non-eligible children with whom they were mixed and who also benefited from the money, did make a measurable gain.[11] Many of the school administrators responsible for these programs had good intentions. Short of segregating the poor children or giving them privileges that their classmates could not share, they found it difficult to help them selectively.

Compared to the rest of the world, the schools of the United States are relatively fair. In Bolivia, for example, one half of all public allocations for schools are spent on 1% of the population. The ratio of educational expenditures on the upper and lower tenths of the population, respectively, are about three hundred to one.[12] Most parts of the world are nearer to the Bolivian than to the United States ratio.

Schools constitute a regressive tax because the privileged go to school longer and because costs increase with the level of schooling. Graduate schools, for example, provide by far the highest student subsidies not only in relative but also in absolute terms. Graduate students come largely from the upper income levels of the society. Nevertheless, students pay almost nothing at this level, in fact are frequently paid, while graduate-school support, even in private universities, comes largely from public funds. Costs in the sciences, for example, run up to several hundred thousand dollars per student per year. An argument is sometimes made that graduate students are exploited as underpaid teachers and research assistants. In a narrow sense this is true, but in the longer view, graduate-school exploitation is merely an initiation fee paid for larger lifetime earnings. At undergraduate levels there is a higher proportion of private expenditure, but even here public subsidies average thousands of dollars per student per year, as compared with hundreds of dollars at the elementary level, where most of the poor children are.[13]

Development economists argue that peasants in India, sharecroppers in Alabama, and dishwashers from Harlem do not need more education until the world is ready to absorb them into better jobs and that these better jobs can be created only by others, who must therefore be given educational priority.[14] But this argument ignores many of the economic, demographic, and political facts of life. Economic growth, where it is occurring, principally bolsters the level of living of the already better off, fattens military and security-police budgets, and supports the markets of more-developed nations. Population is growing so much faster than the rate at which real educational opportunities can be expanded, by means of schools, that deferring the education of the masses merely leaves a more difficult task for the future. On the other hand, few people have voluntarily curtailed birthrates without a minimum of education and social mobility.[15] If there were a monopoly of power in the world, population growth might be curtailed arbitrarily. In the world as it is, to ignore popular demands for education is not only morally indefensible, it is politically impossible except for military governments. For most people, forcing others not to have children would be a completely unacceptable policy in any case.

While children who never go to school are most deprived economically and politically, they probably suffer the least psychological pain. Andean Indians, tribal Africans, and Asian peasants belong to communities that have no schools or have them only for the children of the elite. Their parents and grandparents have never known schools as places they expected their children to attend. They do know, however, what schools imply. Going to school means leaving the traditional life, moving to a different place, laying aside physical burdens for the work of the tongue and the mind, exchanging traditional food, clothing, and customs for those of the larger town or distant city. Parents often prefer to keep the child in the traditional community, bearing the familiar burdens, confined to the enjoyments that primitive means can provide. They know, however, that this implies continuing domination by others, continuing dependence in times of hunger, war, and sickness, increasing distance from those who enjoy wealth, power, and respect. When the choice becomes a real one, most unschooled parents all over the world decide to send their children to school.

These first attenders have a harder time than their older brothers and sisters, for whom the school came too late. They do not last long in school. In 1960, half the children who entered school in Latin America never started the second grade, and half the second-graders never started the third.[16] Three fourths dropped out before they learned to read. They did learn, however, how unsuited they were to school, how poor their clothing was, how bad their manners, how stupid they were in comparison with those who went on to higher grades. This helped them accept the greater privilege and power of the deserving minority and their own relative poverty and political impotence. Yet they were not as ready as their older brothers and sisters to accept the limitations of their traditional lot. A little schooling can induce a lot of dissatisfaction. The more schooling a dropout has, the more it hurts him to drop out. The child who never learns to read can still accept his inferiority as a fact of life. The child who goes on to higher grades may learn that he is really no different from the sons of the mayor, the merchant, or the schoolteacher, except that they have the money or the influence needed to go on to secondary school or college, while he must stay behind for lack of it. For him, it is much harder to accept their getting the better jobs, enjoying the higher offices, winning the more beautiful girls, all because they were able to stay in school longer than he.

A winners' world? If this were all, schools might still be defended; but the winners of the school game are a strange lot. The Ottomans used to geld their candidates for managerial posts. Schools make physical emasculation unnecessary by doing the job more effectively at the libidinal level. This is, of course, a simplistic metaphor. While there is evidence that girls do better in school than boys and that boys do less well the more masculine they are judged to be, this undoubtedly results more from social than from physical factors. The metaphor understates rather than overstates the facts. School domesticates—socially emasculates—both girls and boys by a process much more thorough than mere selection by sex. School requires conformity for survival and thus shapes its students to conform to the norms for survival.[17] If learning the official curriculum of the school were the principal criterion, this might still not be so bad, although it would substitute the learning of what Whitehead and other philosophers of education have called dead knowledge for true learning. The actual survival criteria are much worse. In addition to the wealth or influence of parents, they include the ability to beat the game, which according to John Holt and other perceptive teachers, is mainly what successful students learn in school.[18]

To say that schools teach conformity and also teach students to beat the game is not contradictory. Beating the game is one form of conformity. Individual teachers may be concerned with what children learn, but school systems record only the marks they get. Most students learn to follow the rules that schools can enforce and to break those they cannot. But also, different students learn in varying degrees to conform, to ignore the rules, and to take advantage of them. Those who ignore them in the extreme become dropouts, and learn mainly that they do not belong in school or in the society it represents. Those who conform to the rules become the dependable producers and consumers of the technological society. Those who learn to beat the school game become the exploiters of this society. Those on whom the discipline of the school falls lightly, who easily perform its assignments and have little need to violate its rules, are least touched by school. They are, or become, the social aristocrats and the rebels. This, at any rate, is what happened before schools began to break down. Now all kinds of students join in the rush for the door, while schools engage in a similar scramble to recapture their dropouts by any means.

As late as the turn of the century, schools were still a minor institution and all who were not suited for them and by them had other educational options. Fifty years ago, no country in the world had 10% of its teen-age population in school. Schools have grown so fast partly because they happened to be doing what was important to a technological era when this era began. Their monopoly of education has been achieved as one aspect of the monopoly of technology. The main reason we need alternatives to schools is that they close the door to humanity's escape from this monopoly. They insure that those who inherit influence in a world dominated by technology will be those who profit by this domination and, even worse, those who have been rendered incapable of questioning it. Not only the leaders but their followers are shaped by the school game to play the game of competitive consumption—first to meet and then to surpass the standards of others. Whether the rules are fair or the game worth playing is beside the point.

School has become the universal church of a technological society, incorporating and transmitting its ideology, shaping men's minds to accept this ideology, and conferring social status in proportion to its acceptance. There is no question of man's rejecting technology. The question is one of adaptation, direction, and control. There may not be much time, and the only hope would seem to lie in education—the true education of free men capable of mastering technology rather than being enslaved by it, or by others in its name.

There are many roads to enslavement, only a few to mastery and freedom. Technology can kill by poisoning the environment, by modern warfare, by overpopulation. It can enslave by chaining men to endless cycles of competitive consumption, by means of police states, by creating dependence on modes of production that are not viable in the long run. There are no certain roads of escape from these dangers. There can be *no* road of escape, however, if men remain enthralled in a monolithic secular orthodoxy. The first amendment to the Constitution of the United States was a landmark in history. "There shall be no establishment of religion." Only the terms and the scope of the problem have changed. Our major threat today is world-wide monopoly in the domination of men's minds. We need effective prohibition of scholastic monopoly, not only of educational resources but of the life chances of individuals.

2. WHAT SCHOOLS DO

I learned something in school today.
I signed up for folk guitar, computer programming,
stained glass art, shoemaking and a natural foods workshop.
I got Spelling, History, Arithmetic and two study periods.

So what did you learn?

I learned that what you sign up for
and what you get
are two different things.

Dialogue from Peanuts
Charles Schulz

Schools are supposed to educate. This is their ideology, their public purpose. They have gone unchallenged, until recently, partly because education is itself a term that means such different things to different people. Different schools do different things of course, but increasingly schools in all nations, of all kinds, at all levels, combine four distinct social functions: custodial care, social-role selection, indoctrination, and education as usually defined in terms of the development of skills and knowledge. It is the combination of these functions that makes schooling so expensive. It is conflict among these functions that makes schools educationally inefficient. It is also the combination of these functions that tends to make school a total institution, has made it an international institution, and makes it such an effective instrument of social control.

Custodial care is now so universally provided by schools that it is hard to remember earlier arrangements. Children must, of course, be cared for—if they are really children, that is, and not just young members of the community taking part in its normal productive and social affairs. Most youngsters still get along without special care, all over the world, in the tribal, peasant, and urban dwellings of the poor. It is only mothers who have been freed from the drudgery of food production and preparation who find it necessary to turn the care of their children over to others. This is because of other differences between modern and traditional societies. Older children are taken out of the home by the school, fathers go to work, and grandparents and other members of the extended family are left behind in rural or older urban settlements. Were it not for the school, child care in the modern family would fall exclusively upon the mother. Schools thus help to liberate the modern woman, but only by imprisoning her child and by tying her and her man more tightly to their jobs so that they can support the schools. Women clearly need not only the liberation schools provide but much more. Men and children, however, need liberation too. The same point holds for all who suffer special discrimination. Each group must formulate its own demands and fight its own battles, but unless they also join forces with others they will win only battles, never the war.

Child care costs money, and although schools provide it relatively cheaply, this is where most of the school budget goes.[1] Time studies conducted in Puerto Rico by Anthony Lauria show that less than 20% of a teacher's time is available for instructional activities. The rest is spent on behavior control and administrative routine. Lauria's data support a statement John Gardner once made, long before he was Secretary of Health, Education and Welfare in the federal government of the United States. He said that everything a high school graduate is taught in twelve years of schooling could easily be learned in two years, and with a little effort in one. Since child care is the most tangible service schools provide, and since parents are naturally concerned about the quality of such care, this function has a priority claim on school resources. Other functions must compete for what is left after prevailing local standards of safety, comfort, and convenience have been met.

As children get older, child care paradoxically becomes both more extensive and more expensive. Actual hours spent in school increase, buildings are more luxurious, the ratio of paid adults to students increases, and the salaries of these adults also increase. Where there are no schools, children contribute more to the community and require less support as they grow older.[2] High schools, however, take more of the students' time than primary schools, and cost more, too, while most colleges and universities occupy the full time of the student, at an ever-increasing hourly cost as students progress up the academic ladder. The costs of higher education admittedly cover more than mere custodial care, but at upper as well as lower levels the time students spend in school is an important cost factor. Space is also costly; the commodious college campus, insulated from the non-academic environment, is much more expensive than the neighborhood kindergarten.

Money, however, is the least of the costs of providing custodial care in schools. The really important consequence of packaging custody with the other functions of the school is the extension of childhood from age twelve to twenty-five, and from the sons and daughters of the rich to the youth of the whole society. This, in turn, is only one aspect of the division of modern life into school, work, and retirement.

Children and old people are problems in a society that has no use for them. They are both in danger and in the way, in modern cities. Such cities are no longer needed, however, for civilized living. The physical products people need could be produced economically in widely scattered, highly automated fields and factories. Only the exchange of professionalized services requires cities; while service institutions, such as schools, restaurants, hotels, hospitals, and office buildings, are needed only in cities. Such institutions do not derive a net benefit from the economies of scale, which permit the use of high technology. Even in the case of hospitals the advantages of high technology are offset by the disadvantages of crowding large numbers of patients together.

So long as modern cities survive, institutional provisions will, of course, have to be made for the care of the old and the young. One general solution might be to keep them largely outside the urban sector. Another would be to rehumanize the city, for example by reserving some streets for pedestrians and relaxing the competitive character of urban occupations. Transitional institutions can also be imagined: co-operative child-care centers, specialized apartment buildings for the old and infirm, new kinds of apprentice programs. The concrete alternatives should be an outcome of how people, given a wide range of choices, decide to live. The important point is that technological considerations impose no serious restrictions on these choices. People can have what they want if they can free themselves of habits and preferences, some of which have been frozen into laws and institutions. Schools play a vital role in the transmission of habits and preferences from one generation to the next.

So long as children remain full-time students, they remain children—economically, politically, even legally. While no formal legal sanctions are available against students as such, they can always be deprived of their rights to schooling, and thus to preferred employment and social status. The school schedule remains, also, one of the major supports for age restrictions on the right to vote, to work, to contract, and to enjoy other constitutional privileges and protections. The school itself, as custodian of ever-larger numbers of people, for increasing proportions of their life span, for an ever-growing number of hours and interests, is well on the way to joining armies, prisons, and insane asylums as one of society's total institutions. Strictly speaking, total institutions are those which totally control the lives of their inmates, and even armies, prisons, and asylums do this completely only for certain inmates. Only vacationless boarding schools could strictly be called total institutions, but perhaps the strict definition gives too much attention to the body and too little to the mind and spirit. Schools pervade the lives and personalities of their students in powerful and insidious ways, and have become the dominant institution in the lives of modern men during their formative years.

Studies of prisons and asylums indicate how overwhelmingly such institutions produce the very behavior they are designed to correct. In one experiment, almost all the members of a group of persons diagnosed as hopelessly insane, asylum inmates for over twenty years, were discharged as cured within a few months of being placed in a "normal" environment. In another experiment, a group of persons diagnosed as dangerously insane were allowed to institute self-government among themselves and managed without incident.[3] A similar cure for student unrest would be to stop making children out of people old enough to have children, support them, and fight for them. This would, of course, require other social changes, in addition to the divorce of custodial care from education at the higher levels of schooling, but they are equally necessary changes if society is to survive.

A second function of schools, more directly in conflict with their educational aims than custodial care, is the sorting of the young into the social slots they will occupy in adult life. Some of this sorting occurs at the high school and college level, when students begin to opt for this or that profession or trade and enter special curriculums of one to a dozen years in length for vocational preparation. Even this aspect of job selection in school is wasteful and often personally disastrous. Part of the waste is in the high proportion of dropouts, not only from professional and trade schools but from the professions and trades themselves, frequently after long and expensive investments have been made. Many people find that medicine or teaching is not for them—something they could have found out much sooner and much more cheaply if they had begun as orderlies, nurses, or teacher-aides. Even those who stay in the field of their choice do not escape extensive waste of time and money. According to the folklore of many occupations, the first several years of work are spent forgetting what was learned about the vocation in school. Counseling and other sincere and systematic efforts are made to minimize this kind of waste, but it is doubtful that, even at great additional cost, they can do more than slow its acceleration. The ever-greater separation of school from the rest of life widens a gap that no amount of effort can bridge.

The major part of job selection is not a matter of personal choice at all, but a matter of survival in the school system. Except for members of minority groups, age at dropout determines whether boys and girls will be paid for their bodies, hands, or brains, and also how much they will be paid. This in turn will largely determine where they can live, with whom they can associate, and the rest of their style of life. Within this century, any profession could still be entered at the bottom. Today this is difficult even in countries that provide schools for only a tiny minority. In the United States, it is now hard to become a carpenter without having graduated from high school. In New York City even a garbage collector needs a diploma.

While economic status is largely a function of the level at which a student drops out, power in the society depends more upon the sorting that occurs when high school graduates enter college. Admission to Harvard College practically guarantees access to the groups that will control the major hierarchies of the United States. State and local as well as national hierarchies are the products of the college lottery. Even international agencies are ruled by the graduates of a dozen world-famous universities.

Power and wealth are not everything, of course, but almost everything else depends upon them in many parts of the world. Especially where the school system is dominant, respect, reputation, health, even affection of many kinds, can either be commanded or purchased—if they are not tendered as gifts to those who could order or buy them.

The school system has thus amazingly become, in less than a century, the major mechanism for distributing values of all kinds among all the peoples of the world, largely replacing the family, the church, and the institution of private property. In capitalist countries it might be more accurate to say that schools confirm rather than replace the value-distribution functions of these older institutions. Family, religion, and property have such an important influence on access to and success in school that schooling alters only slowly and marginally the value distributions of an earlier day. Jefferson put it well when he said, in arguing for public schools, that by this means we shall each year rake a score of geniuses from the ashes of the masses. The result of such a process, as the English aristocracy learned long before Jefferson, is to keep the elite alive while depriving the masses of their potential leaders.

Communist countries have, of course, abolished private property, have attempted to abolish organized religion, and have tried to weaken the role of the family. There are few data, unfortunately, to show how much redistribution of values has taken place in these countries, but the general impression is that it is much less than had been expected. One of the strongest supports for this impression comes from the great similarity of school systems in capitalist and communist countries. They perform the same functions and share the same defining characteristics. There is not the slightest doubt that communist schools sort their students into jobs, vocational levels, pay differentials, and power and privilege strata in just the same way as capitalist schools. The only question is whether the prizes go to the sons and daughters of the previously privileged in quite the same degree.

Leaders in communist China are greatly preoccupied with this question. In 1966, schools throughout China were closed in an attempt to make education more egalitarian and down to earth. Mao's own policy statements make clear his desire to rid education of elite control and to make it universally available to the masses. The difficulties encountered in this effort were obviously formidable, however, even for Mao, and it appears that most schools have now reopened with significant but not really fundamental changes in the structure of the system. How much of this compromise was due to ideological and how much to practical considerations is hard to say. The pressures of building a nation in competition with such superpowers as Russia and the United States are tremendous, and schools appear to be an almost indispensable tool for nation building. On the other hand, the educational controversy in China has never abandoned the rhetoric of schools. Despite all the emphasis on universal access, practicality, and revolutionary objectives, the debate always refers to the reform of the school system rather than to its replacement.[4]

It should now be clear why schools have grown so fast. To the masses, and their leaders, they have held out unprecedented hope of social justice. To the elite they have been an unparalleled instrument, appearing to give what they do not, while convincing all that they get what they deserve. Only the great religions provide an analogy, with their promise of universal brotherhood always betrayed.

Betrayal of the hopes of schooling is implicit in the selection function that schools perform. Selection implies losers as well as winners, and increasingly selection is for life. Furthermore, school is a handicap race in which the slower must bear the growing burden of repeated failure, while the quicker are continually spurred by success. Nevertheless, the finish line is the same for all, and the first to get there win the prizes. All attempts to disguise the reality of this situation fail. Parents know the truth, while teachers and administrators are often compelled to admit it. Euphemisms about the transcendent importance of learning and about doing your best are thus self-defeating. It is no wonder, under these circumstances, that some children drop out while others work to win rather than to learn.

Consistently punishing half of the children who are trying to learn what society is trying to teach them is not the worst aspect of combining social-role selection with education. Such punishment is an unavoidable result of the relative failure that half the school population must experience while climbing the school ladder in competition with their more-successful peers. Such punishment can scarcely help but condition this half of the school population to resist all future efforts to induce them to learn whatever is taught in school.

But this is only the lesser evil. The greater is that school necessarily sorts its students into a caste-like hierarchy of privilege. There may be nothing wrong with hierarchy or with privilege, or even with hierarchies of privilege, so long as these are plural and relatively independent of each other. There is everything wrong with a dominant hierarchy of privilege to which all others must conform. Birth into a caste, inheritance of wealth, and the propagation of a governing party are all means by which such a dominant hierarchy can be maintained. In the modern technological world, however, all these means either depend upon or are replaced by the school. No single system of education can have any other result, nor can a dominant hierarchy of privilege be maintained in a technological world by any means except a unified system of education.

If schools continue for a few more generations to be the major means of social-role selection, the result will be a meritocracy, in which merit is defined by the selection process that occurs in schools. Michael Young describes this outcome in his *Rise of the Meritocracy*.[5] His picture of English society fifty years from now is a projection of Galbraith's New Industrial State, with the technocrats in the saddle.[6] His school is a super streaming system, constantly shuffling its students into the channels where their past performance suggests that they belong. The slow students are not kidded in this system; they quickly learn where they stand and where they are going, but they are taught to like it. The quick also know where they are going, and like it so well they end up trying to re-establish a hereditary aristocracy based on merit. This reverse-english twist leads to a happy ending that takes humanity off the hook, but not until the author has made his —and repeated Dante's—point. Any system in which men get just what they deserve is hell.

Schools define merit in accordance with the structure of the society served by schools. This structure is characterized by the competitive consumption of technological products defined by institutions. Institutions define products in a way that is consistent with the maintenance of a dominant heirarchy of privilege and, in so far as possible, with the opportunity for members of the currently privileged class to retain their status in the new "meritocracy."

What schools define as merit is principally the advantage of having literate parents, books in the home, the opportunity to travel, etc. Merit is a smoke screen for the perpetuation of privilege. The ability of IQ tests to predict school performance does not rebut this statement. As Arthur Jensen, the most recent defender of IQ, points out, the intelligence measured by tests is operationally defined as the ability to succeed in school.[7] The significance of Michael Young's book is to show that we would be even worse off if "true merit" were to replace more primitive means of perpetuating privilege.

The third function of schooling is indoctrination. Indoctrination is a bad word. Bad schools, we say, indoctrinate. Good ones teach basic values. All schools, however, teach the value of childhood, the value of competing for the life prizes offered in school, and the value of being taught—not learning for one's self—what is good and what is true.[8] In fact, all schools indoctrinate in ways more effective than those which are generally recognized.

By the time they go to school, children have learned how to use their bodies, how to use language, and how to control their emotions. They have learned to depend upon themselves and have been rewarded for initiative in learning. In school these values are reversed. The what, when, where, and how of learning are decided by others, and children learn that it is good to depend upon others for their learning. They learn that what is worth while is what is taught and, conversely, that if something is important someone must teach it to them.

Children learn in school not only the values of the school but to accept these values and thus to get along in the system. They learn the value of conformity, and while this learning is not confined to school, it is concentrated there. School is the first highly institutionalized environment most children encounter. For orphans and children who are sick or handicapped this is not the case, and the retarding effects of institutionalizing infants is impressively documented.[9] Orphans learn so well not to interfere with institutional requirements that they seldom become capable of making a useful contribution to society. The argument for schools, of course, is that they strike the balance between conformity and initiative that the institutional roles of adult life will require. Some of them do. If all of them did, our chances of escaping the contradictions of modern life would be even less than they actually are.

Other values are implicit in those aspects of curriculum which are alike in schools all over the world. These include the priorities given to dominant languages, both natural and technical. Examples of the first are the priority given to Spanish over Indian tongues in Latin America and to Russian over provincial languages in the Soviet Union. Examples of the second are the priorities given mathematics over music, and physics over poetry. There are obviously good reasons for these priorities, but they are reasons derived from the world as it is, ignoring the claims of both the world of the past and the desirable world of the future. More than this, these decisions reflect not even all of the major aspects of today's world, but preponderantly the balance of political and economic power. Fewer people speak English than Chinese and far fewer speak physics than poetry. English and physics are simply more powerful—at the moment.

Another value implicit in school is that of hierarchy. Schools both reflect dominant values and maintain a stratified world. They make it seem natural and inevitable that hierarchies are inherently correlated and cannot be independent of each other. Schools do not have to teach this doctrine. It is learned by studying an integrated curriculum arranged in graded layers.

Finally, after performing child-care, social-screening, and value-teaching functions, schools also teach cognitive skills and both transmit and—at graduate levels—create knowledge. The first three functions are performed necessarily, because of the way schools are organized. Cognitive learning, although it is declared the principal purpose of schools, occurs only in so far as resources remain after the built-in functions are performed. In urban ghetto schools of the United States, and in rural Brazilian schools, attempting to operate on a budget of fifty dollars per year per child, very little cognitive learning occurs.[10,11] Exceptional teachers can, of course, teach, and exceptional students can learn, within the confines of the school. As school systems expand, claiming an increasing proportion of all educational resources, absorbing more students and teachers and more of the time of each, some true educational experiences are bound to occur in schools. They occur, however, despite and not because of school.[12]

Schools rest much of their case on their claim to teach skills, especially language and mathematical skills. The most commonly heard defense of schools is, "Where would children learn to read?" Literacy has, in fact, always run well ahead of schooling. According to census data, there are always more literate members of a society than persons who have gone to school. Furthermore, where schooling is universal, there are always children attending school who do not learn to read. In general, the children of literate parents learn to read even if they do not attend school, while the children of illiterate parents frequently fail to learn even in school.[13]

In universally schooled societies, of course, most children learn to read in school. Considering when they learn to read and when they begin to go to school, it could hardly be otherwise. Even in a fully schooled society, however, few children learn to read easily and well, although almost all learn to speak easily and well, a skill learned outside of school.[14] Children who do learn to read well, read a lot for their own pleasure, which suggests that good reading—like other skills —is the result of practice. Data on mathematics give even less support to school. Illiterates who participate in a money economy all learn to count, add, subtract, multiply, and divide, while only a small percentage of people in a fully schooled society ever learn much more. Of those who take algebra in high school, only a small percentage do better than chance on an objective test.[15]

There is a body of data collected by Jerome Bruner and his students showing that children who go to school learn concepts that are not learned by those who do not go to school.[16] The concepts studied were those made famous by Jean Piaget, who found that most French and Swiss children learn at about ages six to eight that water poured from a short fat cylinder into a tall thin one is still the same amount of water. Bruner's students found that African bush children who go to schools patterned after the French, learn such concepts much better than similar children who do not go to school. These experiments did not, however, test the effect of relevant learning environments other than school. Until a unique effect of schooling is demonstrated, with everything else controlled, Bruner's data show only that environments affect concept learning and suggest that the more relevant the environment is to the concept the more effect it has.

Another claim is that schools teach the grammar of language and the theories of mathematics, science, and the arts. Undoubtedly they do, but the real question is whether these things are learned in school more than they would be otherwise. Achievement tests give little support to schools. As in the case of mathematics, only a small minority of students do better than chance on the formal aspects of any subject matter. Students who are interested in these matters learn them and those who are not do not. Whether interest in them is stimulated by schools remains very doubtful. Einstein, commenting upon a short period he had to spend in school preparing for a degree examination, said that as a consequence he was, for several years afterward, unable to do any creative work.

The pernicious effect of schools on cognitive learning, of which Einstein complains, is best seen by contrasting the impact of schooling on privileged and underprivileged children. The underprivileged, whose home environments are lacking in the specialized resources schools provide, are relatively unsuccessful in school and soon leave it with an experience of failure, a conviction of inadequacy, and a dislike for the specialized-learning resources of which they are subsequently deprived. The privileged, whose home environments are rich in the specialized resources of the school, who would learn on their own most of what the school has to teach, enjoy relative success in school and become hooked on a system that rewards them for learning without the exercise of effort or initiative. Thus the poor are deprived both of motivation and of the resources that the school reserves for the privileged. The privileged, on the other hand, are taught to prefer the school's resources to their own and to give up self-motivated learning for the pleasures of being taught. The minority of Einsteins and Eldridge Cleavers lose only a little time. The majority lose their main chance for an education.

3. WHAT SCHOOLS ARE

First-hand knowledge is the ultimate basis of intellectual life. To a large extent book-learning conveys second-hand information, and as such can never rise to the importance of immediate practice. . . . What the learned world tends to offer is one second-hand scrap of information illustrating ideas derived from another second-hand scrap of information. The second-handedness of the learned world is the secret of its mediocrity. It is tame because it has never been scared by facts.

> Alfred North Whitehead
> The Aims of Education and Other Essays

It may seem academic to distinguish what schools do from what schools are, but the purpose of the distinction is very practical. The social functions performed by schools are in fact necessary functions. Our argument throughout is that schools perform them badly and that we must discover alternatives to schools. Let us define schools as *institutions that require the attendance of specific age groups in teacher-supervised classrooms for the study of graded curriculums.*

By specifying the age of attendance, schools institutionalize childhood. In schooled societies, childhood is now assumed to be a timeless and universal phenomenon. But children, in the modern sense, did not exist three hundred years ago and still do not exist among the rural and urban poor who make up most of the population of the world. In his *Centuries of Childhood*, Philippe Ariès shows that, before the seventeenth century, children dressed as adults, worked with adults, were imprisoned, tortured, and hanged like adults, were exposed to sex, disease, and death, and in general did not have a special status. The subculture of childhood did not exist.[1] The medieval Church assumed that children, baptized in infancy, reached the age of reason at about age seven; this meant that they were from then on fully responsible for their acts, not only to men but to God. They were capable, that is, either by positive acts or by neglect, of consigning themselves to everlasting torment. In its time this doctrine was not uniquely harsh. Children were treated no more tenderly in the Arab and Oriental worlds and, for that matter, in Africa and America.

All cultures, of course, distinguish infants and sexually immature youth from adults. All cultures have initiation rites that signal entrance into full adult status. All cultures make some distinction between what adults and nonadults may do and have done to them. This is not to say, however, that all cultures have a subculture of childhood that sharply distinguishes the roles of children from those of adults. Children are not expected to work, except at their studies. Children are not responsible for any nuisance, damage, or crime they commit upon society. Children do not count, legally or politically. Children are supposed to play, enjoy themselves, and prepare themselves for adult life. They are supposed to go to school, and the school is supposed to be responsible for them, guide them, and temporarily at least, take the place of their parents. Childhood explains the priority that schools give to custodial care.

Childhood must also be viewed in contrast with modern, preretirement adult life. Childhood and the adult world of work have been drawing apart. While children have been increasingly indulged, preretirement adults—women as well as men—have been increasingly molded to the world of machines and institutions. Childhood has become more child-centered, more indulgent, while adults have been increasingly constrained. The argument for schools is that they provide a necessary bridge from childhood to adult life, that they gradually transform the indulged child into the responsible adult. Schools take the child from his garden, by carefully graded steps, to a prototype of the world of work. They enroll the "complete child" and graduate the "complete man."

As in the case of the school, childhood has probably served a useful purpose. The prechildhood treatment of children was, and is, undesirably brutal. Many of the protections childhood has brought to children are important and necessary—so much so that it is vital to extend them not only to other children, but also to adults. Sexual abuse, under conditions that make consent a farce, is one example. The exploitation of labor under similar conditions is another: one party has the choice of working or starving, while the other has to choose merely between one laborer and another. The enforcement or neglect of conditions that stunt the growth or unnecessarily limit the opportunities of children, or adults, need to be prohibited and prevented wherever they occur. But this is impossible if the indulgence of already indulged children, or adults, is endlessly multiplied. Furthermore, while some protections and indulgences are necessary and good, too many are bad, and we have reached and passed many thresholds in the institution of childhood at which benefits become liabilities. Many of these are obvious and need no argument. One that has already been noted is the extension of the age of childhood to include fully mature adults, so long as these adults remain in school. Much of the protest on the part of youth is related to this fact, as is the resentment by adults of this protest. The case for youth is obvious. Old enough to have children of their own and to fight wars, they are encouraged to do only the latter and are denied the right to participate fully in the economic product of the society. The adult case is also easy to understand. These children, they say, want to remain children and yet to enjoy the privileges of adults. In part, the adults are right. What they forget is that youth did not create the institution of childhood, but were created by it.

Schools, as creators of social reality, do not stop with children. They also create schoolteachers. Before there were schools, there were Greek slaves who safeguarded their young charges in excursions about the city, disciplinarians who kept them at their practice of arms, masters prepared to dispute with them in matters of politics, ethics, and philosophy. Of these, only the disciplinarians survived without major distortion in the early schools. Drill with the pen rather than the sword involved only a change of instrument, and the method was equally effective. Schools stopped being effective in teaching skills when this method was abandoned. The other two roles were totally distorted in their incorporation into school. The caretaker role depended for its educational validity upon not overstepping its bounds. The caretaker/slave had little to say about place, time, or activity. His principal task was to keep his charges within the bounds of safety. The educational value of the activities depended upon student selection and conduct. The master was also transformed into his opposite when placed within the school. His true role was to be questioned and to answer in such a way as to provoke ever-deeper questions. In the school, this role is reversed: the master becomes the questioner and is forced to propound orthodoxy rather than provoke exploration.

Children and teachers do not yet make a school. Without required attendance in specialized space, teachers and children could be a home, a nursery, or a crusade. Required attendance and classroom walls add the time and space dimensions that imply that knowledge can be processed and that children have an assigned time and place. During infancy, they belong in the home. At kindergarten age they begin to belong, for a few hours a day, in school. The amount of schooltime increases with age, until college becomes Alma Mater, sacred or soul mother, the social womb in which the child develops and from which he is finally delivered into the adult world. Classrooms may be varied to include laboratory, workshop, gymnasium, and year abroad, but this is all scholastic space—sanitized, sealed off from the unclean world, made fit for children and for the transmission of knowledge. In this specialized environment, knowledge must be transmitted—it cannot merely be encountered—since in most instances it has been taken out of its natural habitat. It must also be processed, not only to clean it up but also to facilitate transmission.

The transmission of knowledge through teaching, and its processing to fit both school and school children, seems perfectly natural in a technological age that engineers a product to fit every human need. Once knowledge becomes a product, the graded curriculum follows—an ordered array of packets of knowledge, each with its time-and-space assignment, in proper sequence and juxtaposition with related packages. The graded curriculum is the fourth dimension of the school. As in the case of the other defining characteristics, its quantitative aspects are critically important. Childhood becomes a problem when extended over too many years and too many aspects of life. Teaching becomes a problem when students begin to depend upon it for most learning. Classroom attendance becomes a problem when it builds sterile walls around too much of normal life. Similarly, curriculum becomes a problem as it approaches international universality. How much required attendance, classroom teaching, and curriculum is tolerable is not a matter for academic discussion. Free people, choosing freely as individuals and in voluntary groups among an ample array of alternatives, can best make these decisions.

Recent international achievement studies demonstrate quite clearly that the universal international curriculum is now a fact.[2] International norms for mathematics and science have been established. These are admittedly the areas of greatest uniformity, but others are not far behind. Nor is the proliferation of vocational schools, black studies, and life-adjustment classes a significant countertrend, for unless these auxiliary curriculums are tied to the core curriculum, they lead to degrees that are meaningless in the marketplace.

The graded curriculum may well be thought of as the very keystone of a system based on institutionalized childhood, teaching, and classroom attendance. Curriculum unites these other elements and determines their impact on students, teachers, and society.

Learning must, of course, occur in some sequence, and there must also be some correlation between different sequences of learning. These sequences and correlations could, of course, be different for each individual. To some extent they must be, and every educator pays lip service to this idea. Nor, on the other hand, are there many who would insist upon avoiding all attempts to correlate the learning programs of different individuals. For a teacher to impose a preferred order on his subject matter is natural and desirable. It is also desirable that teachers learn from each other and adjust their own order or teaching accordingly. But imposing upon teachers an order not of their choosing is undesirable, and requiring students to follow a particular order, except in deference to a particular teacher, is self-defeating. Only people committed to the idea of a knowledge factory that must run on a prearranged schedule will disagree. The argument that students and teachers must be able to transfer from place to place without losing time is valid only if the synchronized knowledge factory is assumed.

Synchronized learning requires, however, not merely a standard order for each subject but also the coordination of the various subjects. This integrated curriculum creates the school system, which in turn determines the major characteristics of individual schools. Thus the core curriculum of the lower schools is dictated by standard requirements for college entrance. Since the economic value of other curriculums depends upon their relationship to the core curriculum, this curriculum directly or indirectly determines hours of attendance, classroom standards, teacher qualifications, and entrance requirements for the entire school system. Schools that deviate significantly from any of these norms lose their ability to qualify students for college entrance. Even primary school reforms can survive only if they do not threaten the progress of their graduates through the higher levels of the system.

It is by way of the standardized graded curriculum, therefore, that schools become a system that then acquires an international monopoly of access to jobs and to political and other social roles. It can be argued that this monopoly is not by any means complete. Some corporations will still employ the unschooled genius, while Roosevelt and Churchill did not have to pay more than lip service to the schools they attended. But these are exceptions, and if the trend continues, they will not exist for long.[3] Organization by grade, the grading of students, and the maintenance of grade standards; standardized intelligence and achievement testing; promotion within the system, and certification for employment are all justified by a curriculum that determines the internal structure and operations of a school, relationships between schools, and relationships between school and other institutions.

People who want to define any kind of learning group as a school are, of course, free to do so. There are Summerhills and Pacific High Schools, free schools and schools without walls, an increasing variety of reactions to schools as defined and described above. The minor variations last only as long as special people and special funds are being invested in them. The major departures depend even more upon the unique personalities of their founders. Some of these departures will undoubtedly help to blaze the trails that lead from schools to real alternatives. For the present they serve largely to help define the schools that are the only choice of almost a billion children.

Schools treat people and knowledge the way a technological world treats everything: as if they could be processed. Anything can, of course, be processed, but only at a price, part of which involves ignoring certain aspects of the thing and certain by-products of the process. The price of processing people is intrinsically high. They tend to resist. What has to be left unprocessed may be the most important part of the person. Some of the by-products of educational processing are already evident. The greatest danger, however, lies in the prospect of success. A successfully processed humanity would lose the little control of its destiny that has always distinguished man from the rest of the world.[4]

4. HOW SCHOOLS WORK

REMARKS CONCERNING THE SAVAGES OF NORTH AMERICA
Pamphlet by Benjamin Franklin, ca. 1784

Franklin wrote: At the treaty of Lancaster, in Pennsylvania, anno 1744, between the Government of Virginia and the Six Nations, the commissioners from Virginia acquainted the Indians by a speech, that there was at Williamsburg a college with a fund for educating Indian youth; and that if the chiefs of the Six Nations would send down half a dozen of their sons to that college, the government would take care that they be well provided for, and instructed in all the learning of the white people.

The Indians' spokesman replied:

We know that you highly esteem the kind of learning taught in those colleges, and that the maintenance of our young men, while with you, would be very expensive to you. We are convinced, therefore, that you mean to do us good by your proposal and we thank you heartily.

But you, who are wise, must know that different nations have different conceptions of things; and you will not therefore take it amiss, if our ideas of this kind of education happen not to be the same with yours. We have had some experience of it; several of our young people were formerly brought up at the colleges of the northern provinces; they were instructed in all your sciences; but, when they came back to us, they were bad runners, ignorant of every means of living in the woods, unable to bear either cold or hunger, knew neither how to build a cabin, take a deer, nor kill an enemy, spoke our language imperfectly, were therefore neither fit for hunters, warriors, nor counsellors; they were totally good for nothing.

We are however not the less obligated by your kind offer, though *we decline accepting it, and to show our grateful sense of it, if the gentlemen of Virginia will send us a dozen of their sons, we will take care of their education, instruct them in all we know, and make men of them.*

Schools have a hidden curriculum much more important than the one they purport to teach. The purpose of this hidden curriculum is to propagate the social myths, those beliefs which distinguish one society from another and help to hold a society together. All societies have myths, and it is one of the major functions of any educational system to transmit them to the young. Social myths are not necessarily false; in fact, during the golden age of each society they correspond rather well to reality. Social myths are gradually outgrown, however, and in the later stages of a social era they serve largely to sustain beliefs that are increasingly far from what actually goes on in the society.

Let us look at four myths or ideologies that play a prominent role in our society, examine the corresponding realities, and then identify the scholastic rituals that help to bridge the gap between myth and reality. The myths and ideologies selected are those which deal with equal opportunity, freedom, progress, and efficiency.

There is equal opportunity, according to the myths of modern societies, for every man to achieve whatever his ambitions dictate and his abilities permit. This myth asserts that all levels and branches of schooling are open to all and that students are limited only by their dedication and brains. It proclaims that all occupations and social levels are open to anyone with enough drive and the ability to deliver the goods. Increasingly the school is recognized as the major avenue to occupations and social roles, and the openness of scholastic channels is therefore stressed as guaranteeing access not only to academic but to social advancement. This is the myth of equal opportunity, pretending to make everyone's advancement depend solely upon his own personal qualities.

The reality is that all advancement is at the expense of

others. Schools, occupational ladders, and social-class structures are all hierarchies in the shape of pyramids. In school, each higher grade is also smaller. Seldom can grades or levels be skipped. Each successive competition must be survived, therefore, in order to reach the top. In industry the picture is the same. For every president of Standard Oil, ten thousand office boys are left behind.

At what age are the opportunities equal? At birth? It seems unlikely that at birth the son of a president, even though he should begin as office boy, would have no better chance than the son of an office boy. But if not equal at birth, the chances certainly become less equal with every year of life. By the time school begins, no one has irrevocably lost; but as soon as kindergarten is over, grades and IQ scores are recorded, and from then on the door is almost closed for those whose grades and scores are low. This is not because these grades and scores are valid. Even those who believe in them admit that at this age they are highly unreliable.[1] But judgments have to be made. Judgment about which school, which track, which teacher, all judgments that vitally influence the chances for the future. Once the elementary school is passed, it is nonsense to speak any longer of equal opportunity for those who have not done well enough to go on to a good academic secondary school. One trade-school boy in thousands may wind up as head of a construction company, but this is the great exception. In fact, every step up the ladder for one is a step down for another; one can rise to the top only over the heads of thousands. Corresponding to the myth of equal opportunity there is the reality of enforced inequality, with the odds of staying near the bottom many times higher than the odds of getting to the top.[2]

"But of course!" will be the reply. This is the nature of hierarchy. Everyone understands what equal opportunity means. If this is so, then why not tell it like it is. Call it the social lottery. In truth, it would have to be called the loaded social lottery, with each child getting as many chances as his father has dollars. But this would not suit the purposes served by calling it equal opportunity. Everyone is supposed to think he has an equal chance, whether he does or not. It is better for his morale. For the moment, the question is not whether this should or should not be. This is how it is; and the question is, how is it kept that way? How are people induced to believe, or at least act as though they believed, in equal opportunity, when in fact there is no such thing?

They are induced to believe it by ritual progression up the ladder, the school ladder, the promotion ladder, the income ladder, the social-status ladder. As long as people are climbing, it is easy to maintain the illusion that all roads lead to the top. One step at a time, that's how one gets there. The fact that there isn't enough time for the man who gets to the top to touch all the steps on the way is easily overlooked. It makes sense that if you climb, step by step, you get to the top.

There are enough steps so that everyone can climb a few. Grades in school are easy enough at first, in rich countries, and almost everyone passes these early grades. By the time the going gets rough the lesson has been learned: there is equal opportunity, but men just aren't all equal. The job ladder works the same way. Everybody except those who really did badly in school goes up a few steps. Then the intervals get longer. People get a little older. It doesn't matter so much any more.

Everyone's income rises a little, even if he doesn't get promoted—annual increments, each year a little more, and by the time the plateau is reached the illusion is also established that everyone has had a chance. Some are just luckier than others. Obviously this is not the whole truth. But people are induced to believe it by ritual progress up the ladder.

The ideology of freedom is that all men have certain inalienable rights: the right of assembly, the right of petition for redress of grievances, the right to be free from unreasonable searches and seizures, the right to counsel, the right not to bear witness against themselves—i.e., to be free from torture in the first, second, or third degree. The facts are that all over the world the flickering lights of freedom are going out. In the communist world, deviationists and enemies of the people have no civil rights. In the capitalist world, over half of the nations that were democracies twenty years ago now have military regimes, many of which use torture as an everyday instrument of government. The remaining "democratic" governments include South Africa, where "full" civil rights extend only to non-Africans and non-Asians, and then only if they are careful to leave the issue of *apartheid* alone. In the United States, there is also the South, where blacks have the rights that whites deign to give them. In the rest of the country, peoples' rights are increasingly determined by police and national guardsmen. Black Panthers, dissident Democrats, and college students are ever more in danger of having rites instead of rights.

How is belief in freedom maintained in the face of these facts? Largely by the rituals of democratic process. Among other things, the last presidential election in the United States helped people forget the police power used at the Chicago convention by one wing of the Democratic party against the other. Equally, the last national election in France helped people forget the military and police suppression of students and workers that had occurred just a few months before. These dramatic examples, however, are not as important as the daily rituals of democracy in reassuring people about their freedom while domination and suppression are increasing. The professor exhibiting academic freedom by denouncing the establishment, students flaunting hair styles and kicking up their bare feet, sit-ins, paint-ins, sleep-ins, and pot parties—useful as these things are, they serve to reassure people that they are still free when in fact they may not be.

We also have the angry editorial, the enterprising reporter's exposé, the new magazine going the old ones one better, the legislative investigation. Some serve good purposes. Others merely help to maintain the illusion of freedom. With few exceptions, only those who know how to play the game, those already in positions of privilege even though dissident, are able to use the liberty that democratic process provides. Those who are truly deprived have little real access to democratic process. This is one reason Jefferson despaired of orderly reform carried out within the rules. But the rules themselves, ritually followed, disguise the basis for Jefferson's reliance on periodic revolution. Democratic process, in school and society, helps people accept the discrepancy between the assumption of freedom and the facts of domination and suppression. We do not want to lose or underestimate democratic process, but neither do we want to delude ourselves about how much freedom we have and how secure it is. We can protect and extend the limits of our own and other people's freedom only if we see things clearly.

The myth of progress is that our situation is improving and will continue to improve, without any demonstrable limits upon the degree or scope of future improvements. The facts are that we are near the limits at which the atmosphere can absorb more heat or the seas more pollution, near the limits of the earth to support more population, near the limits of the patience of the poor to subsist on the bounty of the rich, near the limits of the rich themselves to either tighten further the screws they have fastened upon themselves or to live much longer with the indulgences they have invented. People who do not want to face these facts say that the problems will be solved by new discoveries and inventions. But the discoveries and inventions of the past have merely brought us to our present predicament. Future discoveries and inventions, similarly applied, can only sharpen this predicament. For regardless of how near or far away the limits are, there can be little doubt that they exist, while the ideology of progress knows no limits. The earth, human population, and human nature are all finite, while progress is infinite. This theoretical problem might not have to bother people if various kinds of progress were in reasonable balance, but they are not. Our ability to kill each other is growing much faster than our productive capacity. The gap between the rich and the poor is widening. Psychological tensions are increasing faster than our ability to deal with them.

The myth of progress is, then, faced with a set of very hard facts, which contradict its assumptions. How are these contradictions reconciled? They are kept from consciousness primarily by the ritual of research—the continuing quest for new knowledge, new insights, new techniques. Research is a very important non-ritual fact, but it is also an important ritual—inducing the belief that new discoveries change the whole picture, that every day is a new day with a new set of rules and possibilities. This is clearly false. Even the most important new discoveries and inventions leave almost everything else unchanged. The invention of breeder reactors stretched the world's supply of fissionable material greatly. Nuclear fusion extends the limits of possible energy sources even more. But these far-reaching developments do not affect the absorption capacity of the atmosphere at all. They have no effect on human population except to threaten its total annihilation. They influence man's ability to think and to govern himself in only the slightest degree. Yet the myth of renewal by research, the belief that major new discoveries can renew all terms of all problems—this myth and belief permit men to avoid seeing the very hard barriers to further progress that in fact exist.

Research is so identified with school that it affects students even more than it does the general population. The greatest impact of research on students comes by way of its effect on curriculum. One of the hallmarks of modern schooling, which separates it most sharply from its own tradition, is that its offerings are labeled as ever new. Yesterday's knowledge is out of date. In Norway, serious thought is being given to declaring degrees more than five years old invalid. The merit of this proposal is that it belatedly recognizes what was always true, that degrees have little validity. Its rationale, however, is that five-year-old knowledge is no longer valid. Every worker will be obliged to come back periodically to the school to refurbish the knowledge he received the last time. Real education is, of course, a lifetime process. But real education and real research are also continuous, work-related processes. Genuine research and education integrate the new into the much greater mass of the old, and this can be done only in the course of work, in the actual discovery and application of the new. The illusion that knowledge must be contemporary to be valid stands between the generations. This conceit of the young is largely the result of ritualized curriculum renewal as practiced by the school.[3]

The myth of efficiency is that modern man has solved his production problems by means of efficient organization, that other men can do likewise, and that most of man's remaining problems can be solved by a similar approach. The fact is, as Kenneth Boulding, the economist, has recently suggested that gross national product, the current measure of a nation's output, is actually a measure of economic inefficiency. Employment in the wealthier countries increasingly follows Parkinson's Law: that employment increases as production decreases. More and more people in the wealthier countries are employed in the service sector, doing things of dubious value. Consider government and corporate bureaucrats, salesmen, advertisers, bankers, accountants, lawyers, teachers, policemen, soldiers, polltakers, social workers, for example. There is no doubt that all these people do something that someone values, but there is also little doubt that as many people despise what they do. Lawyers provide the clearest example; for every winner at law there is a loser. The same thing holds, a little less obviously, for all the kinds of workers listed above and for many other services as well. Many physical goods are also of dubious value—military weapons, pornography, billboards, superjets, automobiles, gravestones, schools, meat products, tobacco, alcohol, marijuana, and fluoridated water—all have varying degrees of opposition. The point is not that work is bad or even, in itself, of doubtful value. It is rather that the value of work depends upon its outcome.

How are the discrepancies between the myth and the facts of efficiency kept from public consciousness? The answer is —through ritualized activity.

Schools learned long ago that the way to keep children from thinking is to keep them busy. Classes, clubs, athletics, cultural activities, homework; the devil finds work for idle hands. This is also how attacks on the efficiency of the school are met—more courses, more degrees, more activities, more enrollment. The graduates of school are well prepared to participate in the activity rites of the outside world: more committees, more projects, more campaigns, more products, more industries, more employment, more gross national product. Not all activity is ritual. But in a nation capable of producing all its agricultural and industrial products with 5% of its labor force, as the United States is, Parkinsonian employment must account for much of the remaining 95%. Ritualized activity must also account for much of the time of adults who are not in the labor force and of students who are in school.

The hidden curriculum of school is dangerous, because it bolsters belief in a sick society—a society dedicated to competitive consumption, which assumes that man wants principally to consume and that in order to consume endlessly he must bind himself to the wheel of endless production. The whole theory of schooling is based on the assumption that production methods applied to learning will result in learning. They do result in learning how to produce and consume —so long as nothing fundamental changes. As means of learning to adapt to changing circumstances, production methods are ridiculous. The need to distinguish these two kinds of learning is kept from our attention mainly by our participation in the scholastic ritual.

5. WHERE SCHOOLS CAME FROM

A single shelf of a good European library was worth the whole native literature of India and Arabia. . . . It is, I believe, no exaggeration to say that all the historical information which has been collected from all the books written in the Sanskrit language is less valuable than what may be found in the most paltry abridgements used at preparatory schools in England . . . I think it clear that . . . neither as the languages of the law nor as the languages of religion, have the Sanskrit and Arabic any peculiar claim to our engagement, that it is possible to make natives of this country thoroughly good English scholars and that to this end our efforts ought to be directed . . . We must at present do our best to form a class who may be interpreters between us and the millions whom we govern, a class of persons Indian in blood and colour, but English in taste, in opinions, in morals and in intellect.

Lord Macaulay
Parliamentary minute on Indian education.

School is a stage in a succession of specialized institutions. Prehistoric rites, myths, and shamans; temples and priestly castes; Sumerian, Grecian, Alexandrian, and Roman schools; monastic orders; early universities, common and grammar schools—all have played a part in the history of the national and international school systems of today. One of the most instructive historical trends is the progressive specialization of content, method, personnel, and location in socially organized human learning. Originally this included much more than what we now call education. Schooling, as everyone knows, includes much less.

Since 1820, archaeology and anthropology have extended the history of man many tens of thousands of years.[1] As far back as the record goes, man has engaged in specialized activities that have much in common with what goes on in schools. Rites and rituals—symbolic practices seemingly unnecessary to the satisfaction of elementary physical needs—have always been part of man's repertoire. As far back as the record goes, we also find evidence of people and places specialized in and for the use of myth and ritual. Some of the earliest records are in just such places: the caves of southern France and Spain, famous for their paintings of prehistoric animals, were apparently used largely for ritual practices. The only human figures included in the paintings are those of shamans, who combined the teacher's role with those of priest, magician, actor, artist, poet, and ideologue. These, at any rate, are roles combined in shamans of existing tribes whose technology and art resemble those of prehistoric man.

Reasoning both from archaeological and modern anthropological evidence, it appears that prehistoric rites shared certain elements of current curriculums. They had an age-specific character, acting out the myths related to birth, adolescence, and death. They explained and celebrated both the everyday and the unusual aspects of the world. They provided activity for idle periods that followed hunt or harvest. They allowed young people to try on adult roles for size.

The line between prehistoric and historic time is marked by the invention of writing, which corresponds roughly in time to the establishment of cities and the great religions. Education emerged out of the practice of worship and government. Its early home was the temple-court, and its early practitioners were specialized priests. Writing itself was probably invented by such specialists. Shamans and priests are thus in the central line not only of the development of teachers and schools, but of the evolution of man. Brain, hand, and tongue; horde, village, and city; magic, religion, art, and science—these are the milestones of man's physical, social, and spiritual development. The priesthoods of city-based religions inherited from their country-cousin shamans a mixture of magic, religion, art, and science, which they began to disentangle and specialize. It is relatively well established that not only writing, but accounting and mathematics, astronomy and chemistry, music, painting, and poetry had their early development in the temple-courts of Egyptian, Sumerian, and other ruling castes, which combined the functions of priest and king.[2] The first formalized teaching of these arts, which still make up most of the modern core curriculum, was a master/apprentice type of teaching. Even earlier, a kind of teaching among equals must have occurred, as one individual shared his discoveries or developments with others. Here is one of the two main roots of the modern school at the very origin of systematic knowledge.

The other, much humbler root makes its first appearance in a Sumerian classroom built to accommodate about thirty children, the discovery of which has led to the speculation that modern modal class size may have been based on the limitations of Sumerian brick and architecture.[3]

Plato and Aristophanes were the first to leave surviving written records of classroom and school.[4,5] These first schools of classical Athens were humble indeed—mere appendages to an educational program that stressed military training, athletics, music, and poetry, and that taught reading, writing, and arithmetic almost as an afterthought. Originally, all education in Athens was tutorial—one aspect of personal relationships that were often erotic as well. As Athens became more democratic, and pupils began to outnumber masters, group instruction gradually replaced the tutorial relationships.

Soon after the first reference in Greek writing to group instruction in literary arts and skills, schools of medicine and philosophy are also mentioned and, soon afterward, a class of schools conducted by Sophist philosophers.[6] These first models of intermediate schools were based on contracts between a master and a group of parents for the instruction of their sons during a three- or four-year period of their adolescence. The Sophists were the first paid teachers of record, and their aim, appropriately, was practical: to make of their students successful men of affairs.

From these meager beginnings in the golden age of Greece there flourished in the Hellenistic colonies scattered by the conquests of Alexander all over the ancient world, school systems prophetic of our own in organization, curriculum, and the age span of students. Children first learned reading, writing, and numbers, and later were taught gymnastics, music, the classics of literature, geometry, and science. The museums of Alexandria and other cities specialized in the teaching of medicine, rhetoric, and philosophy. Most of these centers, patronized largely by Greek families, were privately financed, although a few small cities had public systems, while others were supported by foundations established by wealthy men. One of the main purposes of these schools was to keep alive the Hellenic tradition in a barbarian world. Only a small minority of the Greek population of the Alexandrian world was ever able to take full advantage of them.

The Romans adopted the Hellenistic school and, with minor modifications, used it for the education of their own elite. From the fall of Athens to the fall of Byzantium, therefore, a tiny minority of the world's population was schooled in somewhat the fashion of today. The school was not, however, an important institution in Greco-Roman or in Byzantine times. Its importance to us lies in its role in preserving the memory and some of the culture of ancient Greece until the time of the Renaissance, in Western Europe.

Except in Byzantium, the fall of Rome resulted in a re-union of education and religion that lasted for a thousand years. The educational institutions of the Middle Ages were the cathedral schools and the monasteries. More-specialized in their purpose than the ancient temples, they also had a more-limited educational role; they did, nevertheless, introduce a number of important ideas into the history of Western education. In the earliest Benedictine monasteries, space and time became the parameters of learning as well as of living.[7] Every hour of Benedictine life had its appointed place and task. Adherence to this regimen constituted the good life; no external product or other sign presumed to attest the efficacy of the life thus lived.

The subsequent Dominican and Franciscan orders were based on different principles. Dependence upon the charity of others and identification with the poor replaced the bond-age of time and space.[8,9] As in the case of the Benedictine rituals, begging and the care of the sick and destitute were not designed as training for subsequent living but as a way of life.

The preparatory principle of education was revived by the Jesuits, who in the sixteenth century extended and ration-alized schooling well beyond the limits of Greco-Roman times.[10] The ancient schools had never been more than a small part of an educational program that was a product of tradition rather than of rational forethought. The Jesuits developed a curriculum and an educational method deliberately designed to prepare men not merely for an ordinary life but for a life of unprecedented scope and challenge. At least part of the subsequent growth of schooling is undoubtedly due to their initial brilliant successes. Originally intended for members of an elite religious order, Jesuit schooling was soon extended to the lay elites of the European medieval world.

The rate of this extension and the circumstances under which it occurred are strongly reminiscent of the sudden growth of Greek schooling following the conquests of Alexander. It was the insecurity rather than the dominance of the Greek colonies of Alexandrian times that caused them to build and depend upon schools; it was the insecurity of the Roman Church in the time of Ignatius that accounts for the formation and rapid growth of the Jesuit system of schools. In both cases, the school was seen as a way of preserving a set of values that were losing their dominance.

This chronology of the Christian orders has run ahead of at least one major event in the history of schooling—the foundation of the first medieval universities.[11] Originally devoted primarily to the study of Christian theology, they quickly branched into other fields of knowledge, and long before the Reformation, had become independent institutions in so far as this was possible in medieval Europe. Along with their counterparts in the Moslem world, the universities of Bologna, Salerno, and Paris became the first institutions of any size devoted primarily to the development and propagation of knowledge. They were also, of course, the direct predecessors of modern universities, and thus of the upper layer of the present school system.

Luther and his followers, coinciding so neatly in time with Gutenberg's invention of movable type, gave a vast stimulus to the growth of the lower schools in northern Europe. The large-scale printing of bibles, and the doctrine that salvation was directly derivable from them, made the teaching of reading a moral imperative for Protestants who could afford it. The industrial revolution, coming so closely on the heels of the Reformation, supplied the last condition necessary for the rapid proliferation of schools, providing not only the means, but also a secular rationale, for widespread literacy.[12]

Mere growth in the number of schools did not result in school systems. This dimension of schooling came with the development of the national state. Thus, while public schools first burgeoned in the federated United States, the first integrated systems of schooling developed in France and Prussia. The Prussian development, although later, was the more clear-cut and became an important international model. In Prussia and later in Germany, the development of the school system was coterminous with the development of the national state and was deliberately designed to be one of its principal pedestals.[18]

One aspect of the German school system was the teaching of High German, the language of the school and the unifying language of the state. A common, graded, integrated curriculum was another—designed to serve the military, political, and manpower needs of the nation. A hierarchically organized teaching profession was still another. Most important of all was a carefully thought-out philosophy of education, reflected in school organization, logistics, curriculum, teacher recruitment, teaching methods, and scholastic ritual, and aimed at producing a citizenry tailored to the specifications of the architects of the German national state. No other national system has been so systematically designed. But all nations, in copying to a greater or lesser degree the major features of the German system, have in effect adopted its objectives and its methods. England has perhaps copied them least, but even England's former colonies have followed Germany more than England.

In France, the idea of a national school system first arose partly in opposition to the Jesuits, who in the sixteenth century were among the principal educators of the elites.[14] Despite the suppression of the order in 1763 and the attempts of the legislators of the French Revolution, public schools made little headway. After the restoration of the monarchy, the Jesuits and, at the primary level, the Christian Brothers again played an important role in French education. The educational reform law of 1834 called for friendly relations between Church and state, but the resulting collaboration did not survive the crisis created by the French defeat in 1870.[15] The power of Prussian arms was attributed by many to the efficiency of their national school system, and no effort was spared to initiate a similar system in France.

Public schools in the United States have also had a long

and complicated history. Despite the early establishment of public schools in New England, Pennsylvania, and Virginia, these schools remained for a long time under local control and, except in New England, the privilege of a relatively small minority.[16,17] The original New England schools were quasi universal without being compulsory, because their promoters shared a common conception of man, God, and the world. Even in New England, public schooling became much less than universal with the influx of non-Puritan immigrants beginning early in the nineteenth century. It was, in fact, this lapse from a brief tradition of universal schooling that led Horace Mann to formulate the modern American concept of the public school.[18] Mann's public schools required attendance because persons of different origins, values, and faiths had to be brought to share the common conception that the Pilgrims had taken for granted. These two approaches to universal public schooling illustrate the contradictions that have brought a glorious promise to a dismal end. Thomas Jefferson,[19] Orestes Brownson,[20] and John Dewey[21] saw universal education as the means of equipping men to discover their beliefs and to create their institutions. St. Ignatius of Loyola, Johann Gottlieb Fichte, and Horace Mann saw a similar process as the means of shaping men to the requirements of social goals and institutions assumed to have prior validity.

These ideological strains combined to make public schools popular with both the privileged and the deprived. For the latter, they held the promise of equal opportunity; for the former, the promise of orderly progression under control of the elite. To a degree, both promises were realized, but the contradictions inherent in them have become steadily more obvious as the balance of power has shifted from citizens to the state. In their time, Locke and Jefferson prevailed. John Dewey's more recent effort to put man back in the saddle was merely given lip service.

The organizational, legal, and procedural steps that have welded tens of thousands of nominally independent local school districts and thousands of colleges and universities into a national school system are the logical outcome of a philosophy that views schools as serving national ends. The popularity of such a philosophy, in a century that has seen the number of nations in the world more than tripled, is not surprising. The proliferation of nation-states is clearly one of the major factors in the growth of the international school system. Regardless of reasons, however, the actual development of such a system is one of the amazing facts of human history. Schools are, of course, only one of the technological institutions that have spread from Europe and North America over the rest of the world; but all the others are more easily explained, while none has spread like schooling. Universal schooling has become part of the official program of almost every nation. Every state must have its university, every city its high school, every hamlet its primary school. All nations look to the leading nations for models of curriculum, scholastic organization, and scholastic standards. Capitalist and communist nations compete in schooling their populations, with as little argument about the standards of competition as in the Olympics.

How is all this to be explained? Technology, the profit motive, and the world struggle for power explain most of the growth of international institutions. None of them directly explains the case of schooling. Similarity of constitutions and codes of law can in some cases be explained as the residue of empire and in others as ideological emulation. The spread of hospitals and medical technology can be attributed to the demonstrated efficacy of at least some aspects of modern medicine. There is nothing comparable in modern schooling; schools are as free of the obligation to demonstrate their efficiency as were the Benedictine monasteries.

European world domination during the eighteenth and nineteenth centuries helps to explain the existence of school systems in former colonies. Japanese schools can also be explained in part as a colonial phenomenon, developed as part of a general Western pattern and adopted to avoid colonization. Schools have clearly lagged the most in those parts of the world least influenced by European and American industrialization. Schools have served a major purpose in the consolidation of the new national states that grew out of the wreckage of empire. Schools also serve the elites of these new nations, providing access to international politics, economics, and culture. This does not, however, explain the international popularity of mass education. The real explanation can be traced back to the two previous historic explosions of schooling—the Alexandrian and the Jesuit. As noted, both of these occurred at times when traditional value systems were in jeopardy. This is again the case, but this time the values involved are more basic and more universal than those of Hellas or medieval Europe. In question now are the assumptions of a society based on hierarchy of privilege. The technology that invalidates these assumptions has created the antidote for its own effects: a school system that promises universal access to the goods of technology but denies it in fact.

Modern technology relieves man, for the first time in history, of the need to earn his bread by the sweat of his brow. All preindustrial societies required close to 80% of the labor force to be engaged in agriculture. Now, using existing techniques, 5% of the labor force of a modern society could produce all of the agricultural and industrial goods currently consumed.

Even today, 10% of the labor force of the United States produces 90% of its agricultural and industrial output. And this is almost entirely prior to the application of existing methods of automation and in the face of widespread job-protective pressures from organized labor. Nevertheless, the United States is producing record agricultural surpluses while paying farmers billions of dollars to restrict production. Additional billions of dollars' worth of industrial goods are being produced for commercial export, over and above the value of goods imported. A huge bill of military goods is being produced, while massive space and research programs are underway. If labor and management could agree upon the objective, 5% of the United States labor force could within a very few years produce the goods currently being consumed by the domestic civilian population. This bill of goods, although badly distributed, leaving many people deprived, is nevertheless enormously wasteful in its average composition. It provides an excessive and otherwise unhealthful diet, clothing that is discarded because of style changes rather than wear, so-called durable goods that are made to wear out in a few years, a tremendous packaging component that merely multiplies the pollution problem, and an unbelievable quantity of junk that serves only to relieve the boredom of people whose lives, devoted to the consumption and production of goods and services, have been emptied of real meaning. We would live much better on half as much. Such a society does not require a hierarchy of privilege for any of the reasons that have justified such a hierarchy in the past.

Modern institutions have assumed the burden of maintaining and justifying a continuing hierarchy of privilege. Among these institutions, the school plays a central role. It initiates each generation into the myths of technological production and consumption, the ideas that what is to be consumed must first be produced and that what is produced must be consumed. Not only goods, but services and knowledge itself become commodities. It celebrates the rituals that reconcile the myths and realities of a society that merely pretends to be for all. It prepares men for specialized roles in specialized institutions, selecting and shaping them in terms of both skills and values. By its own hierarchical structure, it accustoms men to accept a single integrated hierarchy of power and privilege.

School qualifies men for participation in other institutions and convicts those who do not meet the requirements of school of not deserving desirable roles in other institutions.

6. INSTITUTIONAL PROPS FOR PRIVILEGE

In less than a hundred years industrial society has molded patent solutions to basic human needs and converted us to the belief that man's needs were shaped by the Creator as demands for the products we have invented. This is as true for Russia and Japan as for the North Atlantic community. The consumer is trained for obsolescence, which means continuing loyalty toward the same producers who will give him the same basic packages in different quality or new wrappings.

Industrialized societies can provide such packages for personal consumption for most of their citizens, but this is no proof that these societies are sane, or economical, or that they promote life. The contrary is true. The more the citizen is trained in the consumption of packaged goods and services, the less effective he seems to be in shaping his environment. His energies and finances are consumed in procuring ever new models of his staples, and the environment becomes a by-product of his own consumption habits.

Ivan Illich, Celebration of Awareness.

Schools are not the only institutions that promise the world and then become the instruments of its denial. This is what churches, to give one plural label to all religious institutions, have always done: packaged the free gift of God, or nature, so that a price could be exacted for it, and then withheld it from people unable or unwilling to pay the price. Churches were remarkable among other institutions, until recently, only for their hypocrisy. Other traditional institutions never pretended to offer a universal gift. Even the prehistoric practitioners of religious magic did not do so. It is the unique mark of the great religions that their founders opened the doors of the spirit to all and that their priests then succeeded in holding these doors open with one hand while charging admission with the other.

Except for churches, traditional institutions were always openly run for the benefit of those who ran them. Courts, kingdoms, armies, empires, and enterprises belonged to their possessors and shared their benefits only with a few and only for a fee. Two non-religious institutions have recently begun to make the claim of offering universal access: first, nation-states and their subsystems such as schools, and second, modern production enterprises.

Something for nothing is not the issue. No religious leader has ever promised something for nothing, but only that the door would open to all those who would follow the path. This is the promise that churches have reneged on in failing to keep their own doors open and that many modern enterprises and public bureaucracies falsely proclaim.

As provision for human needs is institutionalized, the institutions in question define a product and control access to it. They progressively (1) define the product or service that satisfies the need (e.g. schools define education as schooling); (2) induce general acceptance of this definition among the needy (e.g. people are persuaded to identify education as schooling); (3) exclude part of the needy population from full access to the product or service (e.g. schools, at some level, are available to only some people); (4) pre-empt the resources available for satisfying the need (e.g. schools use up the resources available for education). The above generalizations hold for health, transportation, and many other kinds of human needs, as well as for education.

Health is progressively defined and conceived as access to the services of physicians and hospitals and to the products of the drug industry. This access is notoriously unequal. The cost of hospitals, doctors, and drugs is increasing faster than the resources available to pay for them. It can also be argued that the health of mature populations, those whose birth and death rates are converging, is getting worse as expenditures for hospitals, doctors, and drugs increase. We are merely achieving a longer sick-life by means of these expenditures. People may indulge themselves more as more remedies become available, but if more resources were devoted to preventive measures, sickness as well as death rates would decline.

In the case of transportation, the facts are even clearer. The private automobile has almost displaced its competitors in many countries. In the United States, saturation is reaching the point of declining utility, even for car owners. Yet half the adult population remains without dependable access to a private car and has a harder time getting transportation than if cars had never been invented. Even in Los Angeles, which reputedly has more cars than people and is drowning in its own exhaust, there are as many old and young people who cannot or are not allowed to drive as there are qualified drivers.[1] These people, even those who belong to families that include qualified drivers, must wait upon the convenience of their chauffeurs, or vice-versa.

Provision for a category of human need is institutionalized to the extent that there is a prevailing standard product or service, a standard production and distribution process, and a standard price (with the concept of price including all significant conditions of access). It is worth noting that the people priced out of the market are convinced not only of their un-worthiness to participate in it, e.g. their inability to pursue college studies or to wear stylish clothes, but also of their un-worthiness to participate in the privileges that college educa-tion and stylish clothes imply.

Until democracy was popularized and technology institu-tionalized, claims of universal political and economic partici-pation could not be made. Now such claims sound plausible and are widely believed. The makers of these claims come with specific products designed to meet specific needs. They elaborate a package that becomes ever more complex, more exclusive of access, and more expensive. More basic, however, than product elaboration is the identification of need with product. The words education and school, health and hospital, automobile and transportation become inseparable. People forget that there were educated men before there were schools, healthy men before there were hospitals, and that men walked and rode before they drove or flew.

As institutions grow, more and more people accept the iden-tification of need and product. In medieval Europe, only the Jews and the Moors failed to identify salvation with the Cath-olic Church. Women, who throughout history have borne their babies in the fields, are now recruited into maternity wards. Peasants who have never seen schools vote for the candidates who promise them.

Women and peasants are not irrational. They see that those who go to hospitals and schools are better off. While they also see that those who are better off have greater access to schools and hospitals, they frequently confuse cause and ef-fect. This is not surprising, since the most astute researchers are often unable to disentangle them. Only in rare cases can the efficacy of a medical or educational treatment be con-clusively demonstrated.

Product elaboration effectively prevents universal access, even to the simplest products. Pins and needles are packaged in ever-fancier collections. Salt becomes a monopoly and a form of tax. One of Gandhi's first struggles in India was against the salt monopoly maintained by the British government.[2] The Italian government still maintains a monopoly on salt except in Sicily, where salt is produced. What happens to schools, hospitals, and automobiles is common knowledge; people are priced out of the market not only directly but by increasingly complicated rules—drivers' licenses, entrance examinations, insurance requirements. There are good reasons for all the rules, but their proliferation tends to shrink the proportion of qualified consumers.

There are, of course, opposing processes. Because of consumer credit, rising incomes, growth of public systems of schools and hospitals, etc., net access to modern institutions may even gradually increase. Beyond question, however, the excluded portion of the population, even if declining in number, gets steadily worse off as the monopoly of an institutional product is established. No resources remain for alternative products. As school budgets grow, support for educational alternatives must decline. Not only do school dropouts find progressively fewer educational resources, they also have fewer job opportunities. And finally, they have fewer excuses. As automobiles increase in number, there are fewer trains and buses; those which survive are more expensive, less satisfactory, and less profitable.[3]

During the past decade, the number of new owners of automobiles throughout the world increased by no more than twenty-five million. Perhaps a roughly equivalent number enjoyed for the first time the benefits of modern medical services. The number of school children may have increased by a hundred million. But the population of the world increased by over half a billion during the decade, so that the numbers without any of these services increased much more than the numbers with them. Even more were priced out of the market during this period. The price of automobiles increased substantially, while the cost of medical services and schools multiplied several times. Meanwhile, per-capita income, on a world-wide basis, rose very little. Even if there had been no population growth, and other things had remained equal, more people would have been priced out of the markets for modern goods and services during the 1960s than were added to them.

Nor can the above figures be written off by labeling the sixties as a bad decade, in which major institutions did not function as they are supposed to. In a world dominated by competition for privilege, there is no other way in which institutions can function. The already privileged continue to demand better schools, better hospitals, better cars. As the number who enjoy these commodities increases, there are ever more people to be supplied with ever more-expensive packages, making it increasingly difficult to extend similar privileges to an ever-widening ring of a growing population. Even without population growth, the above factors—plus ecological limits—might make it impossible ever to universalize even the current standards of living of Europe and America.

The excluded are not the only, perhaps not even the principal, sufferers. Those who participate, but to a limited degree, feel sharper pain. Imagine the anguish of pious folk whose relatives languished in purgatory while those of more fortunate neighbors were professionally prayed into heaven. Imagine the torment, today, of persons whose relatives die because donors of kidneys and hearts are co-opted by those who can pay. The fortunate feel no pain but they may be hurt worst of all, for they get hooked on a game that has no end and that no one can win. The struggle of the rich against old age and death is a grotesque example. Much worse, if less macabre, is the status scramble, which as it spreads to more products and more people, poisons the air, the water, and the earth and sucks the very meaning out of life. A squirrel in a rotating cage is no more hopeless or ludicrous than the Smiths and the Joneses trying to keep up with each other.

When Veblen wrote his account of conspicuous consumption over seventy years ago, it was part of a theory of the leisure class.[4] Confined to this class, competitive consumption may have been morally offensive, but it remained socially tolerable. Extended to the masses, competitive consumption destroys man, his society, and his environment. A limited leisure class could consume at the expense of the masses. Open-ended consumption can occur only at the cost of the consumer. But man can no more live in a squirrel cage than can a squirrel. Society cannot survive class conflict stoked to increasing heat by international warfare, universal advertising, and competitive schooling. The world cannot absorb the waste it now receives, let alone the amount implied by present trends.

One critically important aspect of the competitive consumption of institutionalized products is competition among nations. The early products of modern institutions—people as well as things and services—were exported from Europe to the New World and to European colonies, thus providing opportunities for all members of the populations of these European nations. Those who could not attend the new schools or buy the new goods could migrate to the New World, be drafted as soldiers to police the colonies, or take over the land of those who left. They were therefore priced out of the new markets only temporarily. The sons of these conquerors of new land became, in fact, the pioneers of new levels and types of human consumption. The presently developing nations are not, with some exceptions, able to displace or conquer weaker peoples. Far from being able to involve their total populations in export trade, migration, or conquest, they are instead required to compete inside their domestic markets with imports of foreign products, including manpower. Far more of the population of underdeveloped nations, compared with those which developed earlier, is priced out of schools, hospitals, and modern transportation. This part of the population is progressively alienated from the elite of its own nation, from those who do have access to the products of modern institutions, foreign or indigenous. The alienated masses become, in turn, a demographic drag, an economic liability, and, ultimately, a political opposition.[5-10]

Most institutions continue to serve the interests of their inventors and at the same time the interests of those who were originally peripheral to them, only at the cost of an even more-peripheral group.

In the days when political empires were the salient institutions, the above statement would have excited no interest. The privileges of Roman citizenship were extended only as additional territories were conquered. Marx applied the principle to capitalist institutions. We merely generalize the principle to other institutions and possibly free it of dependence on the notion of deliberate exploitation. Most of those attempting to universalize schooling and hospital care sincerely believe that they act in the interest of the as yet unschooled and uncured. Earlier missionaries, conquerors, and even traders frequently acted with the same conviction.

The difficulty is that we are the prisoners of our institutions rather than their masters. Seldom do we consciously design them, and when we do, we can scarcely finish the process before bowing down in reverence. So in their thrall are we that we tremble lest we lose them inadvertently and fall helplessly back into barbarism. Actually this fear is largely confined to the privileged, and what we really fear is that the specific bases of our own privilege might get lost in the institutional shuffle.

There is, then, a political as well as a psychological aspect of the difficulty. There are those who benefit from present institutions and who consciously desire to preserve them. Among these are owners, managers, political leaders, and other holders of power, including the common citizens of privileged nations. But many with power have no conscious desire to monopolize it, and many over whom power is wielded give in to the illusion rather than the reality of power. Man cannot free himself from existing institutions without struggle, but neither will struggle avail unless preceded by imagination and invention. One of the major problems is that the developed nations now have an effective, if not necessarily deliberate, monopoly of the means of modern invention.

Theories of political revolution are not sufficient. Such theories assume that if a new class gains control, the society will change in accordance with the values of this class as expressed in its ideology. In practice, we see that a spate of revolutions throughout this century has left most of the specialized institutions that constitute societies intact. The schools and hospi-

tals of communist states are no different from those of capitalist states. Even the recent revolution in Cuba is attempting
to extend health and education services to the masses largely
by means of traditional school and hospital systems. The agricultural and industrial institutions of communist and capitalist
states tend to converge, despite great efforts on both sides
to make them different. According to prevailing theory, technology provides the force that defeats these efforts, but technology scarcely explains the case of the school, of the church,
of the family, or of many other institutions that have, temporarily at least, defeated the efforts of revolutionary governments to change them.

Yet there is ample evidence that institutions are by no
means eternal. During this century, monarchies have disappeared, political empires have broken up, churches have lost
their power if not their membership, labor unions have risen
and declined, entrepreneurs have been replaced by managers
and technicians, major industries have disappeared and been
born. Many of these changes are almost totally unexplained;
others, especially the political changes, have resulted from
specific plans, sometimes based on a general theory of political
revolution. Man has shown himself capable of creating and
destroying institutions, on a planned or an unplanned basis,
with or without theory. At the same time, he remains the pris-
oner of his institutions to an almost unimaginable degree. He
can break his thralldom only by first understanding it thoroughly and then by deliberately planning the renovation and
replacement of his present institutional structures. This is a
necessary—not a sufficient—condition. Struggle cannot be
avoided, but struggle without adequate prior understanding
and planning has again and again proved futile.

Understanding and effective action will require a general
theory of institutional change. We must develop conceptual
tools for the analysis of institutions in order to understand the
historical process by which they were introduced, the socio-
logical process by which they became acceptable, and the
limitations that they now place on the search for alternatives
(not only limitations of power and resources, but also limita-

tions upon the creative imagination). We must develop a language in which we can speak with precision about the needs of modern man—a language freed from the one that is shaped by those institutions men have come to accept as the definers of their needs.

7. ARE DEMOCRATIC INSTITUTIONS POSSIBLE?

If we continue to believe that the goals of the industrial system—the expansion of output, the companion increase in consumption, technological advance, the public images that sustain it—are co-ordinate with life, then all of our lives will be in the service of these goals. What is consistent with these ends we shall have or be allowed; all else will be off limits. Our wants will be managed in accordance with the needs of the industrial system; the policies of the state will be subject to similar influence; education will be adapted to industrial need; the disciplines required by the industrial system will be the conventional morality of the community. All other goals will be made to seem precious, unimportant, or anti-social. We will be bound to the ends of the industrial system. The state will add its moral, and perhaps some of its legal, power to their enforcement. What will eventuate, on the whole, will be the benign servitude of the household retainer who is taught to love her mistress and see her interests as her own, and not the compelled servitude of the field hand. But it will not be freedom.

If, on the other hand, the industrial system is only a part, and relatively a diminishing part, of life, there is much less occasion for concern. Aesthetic goals will have pride of place; those who serve them will not be subject to the goals of the industrial system; the industrial system itself will be subordinate to the claims of these dimensions of life. Intellectual preparation will be for its own sake and not for the better service to the industrial system. Men will not be entrapped by the belief that apart from the goals of the industrial system—apart from the production of goods and income by progressively more advanced technical methods—there is nothing important in life.

John Kenneth Galbraith,
The New Industrial State

In the admitted absence of an adequate language of institutions, the hypothesis that institutions can be democratic may appear premature. The hypothesis of this chapter, however, is that institutions can be identified in which the tendency toward domination can be restrained[1] and that encouragement of this kind of institution can foster the growth of a just and democratic society.

Institutions are so identified with hierarchy, control, privilege, and exclusion that the very notion of democratic institutions seems strange. Jeffersonian democracy was based on the relative absence of large institutions, and came to grief with the growth of corporations and public bureaucracies. According to Galbraith and others, today's technology requires large institutions. As indicated by the preceding quotation, Galbraith's theme in *The New Industrial State*[2] parallels in many ways the argument of this chapter. His argument is much more detailed and much more carefully qualified; without the support of his documentation, the positions taken here would be much less tenable. Galbraith does not, however, suggest an institutional dichotomy of the type outlined in this chapter. In *The Affluent Society*,[3] which is in a sense a companion volume to *The New Industrial State*, Galbraith suggests the need for a massive shift of resources from private to public enterprise. Again, the major difference from the argument of this chapter lies in Galbraith's much greater caution, coupled with an immensely greater documentation of his assertions. For Galbraith, all hope seems to lie in a shift in basic values. In the absence of such a shift, little else is possible. He may be right. But this chapter suggests that if such a shift should begin to occur, an appropriate program of institutional development might lead to something better than mere battle between institutional and humanistic social goals.

Historically there have been at least quasi-democratic institutions: the Greek city-state, the New England town, the Jeffersonian republic; some of the early temples, churches, and religious fraternities; the Chinese market networks.[4] There are also some modern institutions that seem to serve democratic purposes: postal systems, telephone exchanges, and road networks, for example. If Chinese markets and road networks do not appear to qualify for institutional status, this is at least partly because of the way we have been trained to think about institutions.

The history of institutions is a history of domination. Armies, temples, courts, and empires established the institutional mold, and despite exceptions, their pattern has continued to determine man's thinking almost to the point of defining deviations from this pattern as non-institutional. Even people who admit that an organization that is not hierarchical or exclusive might be called an institution, will argue that hierarchy and selective membership increase institutional efficiency. They probably do—for purposes of domination. Institutions that are better at dominating their members may also be better at dominating their rivals. Despite Pericles' eloquent claim for the superiority of Athenian democracy, Sparta won the war. The relatively democratic Greek city-states were later conquered by much less-democratic Rome. The record begins to get fuzzy with England's triumph over Spain and with the results of the two world wars. But even English history credits the better discipline of her navy, obtained partly by means of the lash, and the record is not yet closed on the battle between dictatorship and democracy. Currently the loudest clamor for control comes from the leadership of the democracies.

Admission that large, hierarchically controlled institutions may be better at dominating others will not satisfy the adherents of hierarchy. They claim greater productive efficiency as well. This is a little like claiming that big sharks have more efficient digestive systems than little sharks because they succeed in eating them. Is General Motors more productive because it is bigger, or bigger because it is more productive? The answer is neither. It is bigger because it is the product of a merger; its size gives it the resources to dominate other companies that remain independent. It is not, in general, a more efficient producer, or it would not buy so many large and small components from smaller companies. Its size does help it to dominate the market, which in turn permits some economies of scale in production. General Motors is currently the most efficient player of the game in which it is engaged, just as the United States and Russia are currently the leaders in the world struggle for domination. No one would claim that both of these nations are models of efficiency in all other respects.

Consider American Telephone and Telegraph, in contrast with General Motors. It is just as technical, just as profit-oriented, just as large as General Motors, but there is a great difference in what the two companies do for and to their clients. The telephone company installs a phone and there it stays, whatever its age, shape, or color, unless the customer, for special reasons of his own, decides he wants a different model. The telephone subscriber pays a few dollars a month and, unless he has teen-agers, forgets about his phone until someone calls him or he wants to call someone else. The telephone doesn't have to be washed, waxed, or serviced, except rarely, requires no insurance, and is not liable to theft. It is not, on the other hand, a source of pride or envy, of concern or comfort, of thrill or trepidation. It is just there, in case it is needed to call next door or halfway around the world, imposing no constraints on what is said and not intruding itself in any way into the use that is made of it. Anyone who has a dime or a friend or an honest face or an emergency can use it, even if he can't afford or doesn't want a phone of his own. And the essential service the user gets, the value it has for him, has nothing to do with what he pays or who he is. Clearly, people who are better off are more conveniently served, but the telephone network is essentially democratic—so long as it serves individuals rather than computers, corporations, or military systems.

How different the Cadillac or Chevrolet, not so much owned as owning its possessor. Long before we purchase, the model, color, style, horsepower, power steering, power windows, to say nothing of other options, dominate the family council. Subsequent payments dominate the family budget as much as the new car dominates family life. Triumphs and tragedies succeed each other in rapid succession as it passes or fails one test after another. Utility is our last concern. We join car clubs to avoid exposing the new member of the family to the dangers of the parking lot. Gasoline mileage is merely a point of debate with the neighbors. Emission of lead and other air-borne poisons we do not even think about.

Human nature? Perhaps. But elsewhere people compete on horses, or on foot, or with sticks or stones, without surrendering their lives (including employment, taxes, education, and the condition of the air, water, and land on which they live) to the producers of these horses, sticks, or stones. And yet, human nature is involved. The automobile, like the modern house or household utility, is too big a toy to be resisted. Offered, even in exchange for submission to its supplier, it is as hard to resist as were the early cults with their idols, incense, and temple prostitutes. Life is dull, and what else is there to relieve the tedium?

This is one of three traditional ways of dominating men. The others are force and the withholding of necessities. Force is relied upon mainly between nations. Necessities are withheld to insure the services of the lower classes. The grown-up plaything game is used to keep the palace guard in line. International competition, interclass competition, and interpersonal competition are all related. The first requires the military institution, the second the police and penal institutions, and the third requires General Motors. What these institutions have in common is the advantage they try to establish for one group or individual over another. What all forms of advantage have in common is that they exact a price for the advantage as well as for the product that provides it. When the advantage is permanent, this price must be paid continuously. When the advantage is on all counts, the price is total. The point is made elegantly in the Faust legend, and the theme appears throughout human mythology. It provides the touchstone for distinguishing democratic from dominating institutions.

Democratic institutions offer a service, satisfy a need, without conferring advantage over others or conveying the sense of dependence that institutions such as welfare agencies do. They take the form of networks rather than production systems—networks that provide an opportunity to do something rather than make and sell a finished product. Public communication and transportation systems are examples, as are water works and sewers, electricity and gas distribution systems, and general markets that facilitate the flow of various kinds of goods. Public utilities are democratic institutions if they are truly public and provide something really useful.

Everyone has access to a true public utility, either free of charge or at a fee everyone can afford. Access is at the option and initiative of the user, who may also leave the service when he wishes. The most useful products, such as electricity or water, can be used for a variety of purposes. So can roads or the mails. Public utility networks show true economy of scale. The bigger they get and the more of the population they serve, the more useful they are for everyone. Water and sewer systems, which might seem to be exceptions, are seen not to be when public health is considered. Superhighways, as opposed to road networks, are false public utilities. They are actually the private preserves of car owners, built partly at public expense. Utilities serve basic, universal needs. Everyone needs water, power, communication, transport, food, raw materials, a place to exchange fabricated products, and many other things. Nevertheless, basic needs are limited. They cannot be indefinitely multiplied. They can, therefore, be satisfied without exhausting all available time, labor, raw materials, and human energy. After they are satisfied, there are things left for people to do, if and when they like, and there are remaining resources for doing them. The managers of democratic institutions can and must be largely responsive to the expressed desires of their clients.

Institutions that confer or maintain advantage over others fit a description almost diametrically opposed to that above.

They tend to be production systems rather than networks. If networks are involved, they have the secondary purpose of distributing a particular product. Access is limited, and access costs are frequently high. Once on, it isn't easy to get off; participation is often either obligatory or addictive.[5] The product tends to be specific, elaborate, and all-purpose. There are important diseconomies of scale. At some point, extension of the service to new clients becomes a disservice to former clients. The needs served are not basic but at least partly induced. Once induced, however, these needs are open-ended and can never be fully satisfied. Surfeit leads to excess rather than to satiation. Dominating institutions tend, therefore, to become total, to exhaust the life space of human beings and the life-sustaining capacity of the biosphere. The managers of dominating institutions must take and maintain the initiative. Clients must be seduced, manipulated, or coerced. True initiative or choice on the part of clients tends to disrupt the maintenance requirements of dominating institutions.

Most actual institutions fit these opposing prototypes only partially. Some fit fairly well, including certain public utilities on the one hand and military establishments, prisons, and asylums on the other. Most products, services, and institutions fall somewhere in between. Automobiles, modern houses, and home appliances are not merely pawns in a status game, but are also useful. Making long-distance calls on credit cards, on the other hand, may be pure oneupmanship. The management of the telephone company and its institutional advertising differ little from those of General Motors, which also produces buses as well as private cars. The buses are, however, almost incidental. The policies of General Motors and its role in the society are determined by the private automobile, considered not primarily as transportation—as Henry Ford viewed the Model T—but as status symbol. With the development of the video-phone, the telephone company could easily embark on the same route. A video-phone is not for everyone, and might seem to require private viewing space. This in turn could lead to elaboration not unlike that which has afflicted the automobile. If the choice were left to management, there is little doubt that AT&T would follow the route of General Motors. The management of a true public utility must be at the service and command of its clientele. The management of a dominating institution must manage its clientele as well as its personnel. The choice is a fateful one. It is, hopefully, not too late for the public to choose.

The choice is not between high and low technology. It is not necessarily between private and public management, of either "public" utilities or "private" factories for necessary products. It is a choice of shopping lists, of the kinds and varieties of products that will be available. An unlimited market basket for the rich is not compatible with freedom for either the rich or the poor. But this metaphor is inexact. The "unlimited" market basket can be filled only with those products of high technology that enough people can be induced to buy. It can, of course, be filled with custom-made products for those who can afford them, but even these will be the products of an inherited artisanship living on the past. A vigorous artisanship cannot survive in unrestricted competition with high technology. The choice ultimately is between two completely different styles of life. One is egalitarian, pluralistic, and relatively sparse in the kinds of products and services it provides. People have to do things for themselves, but have time and freedom to do what they want. The other kind of life is based on a unified hierarchy of privilege maintained by international, interclass, and interpersonal competition. The kinds of competition are limited and highly structured, but the prizes are relatively glamorous, at least on the surface.

It may seem idealistic in the extreme to believe that people who have the second option already in their hands will voluntarily exchange it for the first. Yet there are signs that this could happen and the choice may not be entirely voluntary. Pollution of the environment, pressure from the underprivileged, and the horrors of war may help to decide the issue. But blind forces cannot achieve intelligent solutions of issues. Only intelligence can do that. This is why education is so important, and why it cannot be left to schools.

Schools are themselves dominating institutions rather than

opportunity networks. They develop a product that is then sold to their clients as education. Concentrating on children gives them a less-critical clientele, to which they offer the prizes that other dominating institutions produce. Parents want these prizes for their children, even more than for themselves, and can be sold a rosy future even more easily than a current illusion. Seen at a distance, the fallacies of competition are harder to perceive clearly. Foreigners can have what we have if they will follow the course we have followed. Workers can achieve our standard of living if they will educate themselves to earn it. Our children can have what we couldn't have if they will prepare themselves to produce it. These propositions sound so plausible and yet are so patently false when viewed in perspective. An open-ended consumption race must always result in a hound who gets the rabbit, a bunched pack in the middle who get some of the shreds, and a train of stragglers. This must be the outcome in terms of nations, of classes, and of individuals. Schools not only cloud this perspective, they actively foster the illusions that contradict it. They prepare children precisely for interpersonal, interclass, and international competition. They produce adults who believe they have been educated and who, in any case, have no remaining resources with which to pursue their education.

Schools will have to be replaced by opportunity networks that provide universal access to essential educational resources —including things and people.

8. NETWORKS OF THINGS

An Expedient was therefore offered, that since Words are only Names for Things, it would be more convenient for all Men to carry about them, such Things as were necessary to express the particular Business they are to discourse on. And this Invention would certainly have taken Place, to the great Ease as well as Health of the Subject, if the Women in Conjunction with the Vulgar and Illiterate had not threatened to raise a Rebellion, unless they might be allowed the Liberty to speak with their Tongues, after the Manner of their Forefathers: Such constant irreconcileable Enemies to Science are the common People. However, many of the most Learned and Wise adhere to the new Scheme of expressing themselves by Things; which hath only this Inconvenience attending it; that if a Man's Business be very great, and of various Kinds, he must be obliged in Proportion to carry a greater Bundle of Things upon his Back, unless he can afford one or two strong Servants to attend him. I have often beheld two of those Sages almost sinking under the Weight of their Packs, like Pedlars among us; who when they met in the Streets would lay down their Loads, open their Sacks, and hold Conversation for an Hour together; then put up their Implements, help each other to resume their Burthens, and take their Leave.

Jonathan Swift, Gulliver's Travels

There are things with general and things with special educational significance. Those of special educational value are again of two kinds: those which embody symbols and those which produce, translate, transmit, or receive information encoded in symbols. All objects serve as means of communication, but as Swift points out, some serve it better than others. Among those which serve it best are records, books, tapes, anything used for the storage of symbols. Records are relatively so easy and cheap to store and to keep that they can be organized for quick access enormously more efficiently than the things they represent. This is the virtue of human brains, but also of computers, libraries, microfilm stores, and the like. Large collections of records, such as central libraries or national archives, are like collective memories serving societies as brains serve individuals. Further organization of such record collections, by means of computers, is certain to increase their utility greatly and to warrant the comparison with human brains. Effective access to records is sure to become even more necessary to the educated man than it is today. Even today, records are very significant extensions of educated brains. Much that could be kept in human memory is deliberately passed on to these supplementary memory systems.

One of the things that makes almost unlimited universal education potentially so cheap is the great economy with which record systems of many types can now be organized for very rapid access by almost unlimited numbers of people. Anyone who learns to use these systems, for which only elementary skills are needed—at least for certain levels of use—is then capable of carrying on his own education to almost any degree. This has always been true for people who knew how to read and to find books. The new development will simply make it easier. It may be worth noting that this has also always been true for anyone who knew how to observe and to find information. Reading merely made things easier, just as computers now do. They make things so much easier, however, that education can now become universal.

The quality of this education will depend only upon the quality and completeness of the records that are available to the public. Information upon which corporate and national advantage presumably depends will not be available. Neither will other information deemed vital by some groups for the maintenance of their advantage over others. These are problems that organization alone cannot solve.

Libraries are partial models for the organization of records and similar objects. Only an extension of the library system is necessary to enable these kinds of educational objects to be located and placed at the disposal of learners. But the scope of the extension required is very great. Libraries do not yet take full advantage of the ease and economy with which most records can now be reproduced. They are, of course, seriously handicapped by property rights and consequent restrictions on reproduction. These restrictions and the novelty of cheap reproduction methods account for the carry-over of the custodial tradition, which opens libraries to the charge of being more concerned with their records than with their clients. This tradition will have to be overcome, as will the tradition of serving an elite rather than the general public. The reading public is an elite, and because libraries were founded on books, an elite as well as a custodial tradition has limited their educational scope. It might not even be a good idea to use the name library in the network of educational objects that must become one of the major institutional alternatives to schools.

In addition to vastly expanded directories and repositories of all kinds of records, we need effective access to objects that have special value in the transmission of information. Among these are the instruments that play records, produce them, or transmit their message. Books are among the few records that do not require special decoders. In the production of books and papers, however, instruments are indispensable: pencils, typewriters, mimeograph machines, or presses. Universal access to these instruments is just as important as the ability to read what has been written. This is why freedom of the press was included in the American Bill of Rights. Its original purpose was to protect the rights of common people such as Thomas Paine to make their ideas public; only later did it become primarily a protection of the commercial press.

Most records other than books require instruments for their production and also for their use. Musical instruments and microphones may be needed to produce and record sound, and record players to hear it. Typewriters and computers are needed for the production and reading of punch cards, tapes, disc-packs, and other types of computer records. Cameras and projectors are another pair of basic instruments, which can be combined with telescopes, microscopes, and many other devices, and can use television or telephone lines as transmitting devices. Then there are simpler kinds of materials for producing records, such as paint and brushes, knives and chisels, knitting needles and string—a great variety of common tools and materials.

Message coding and decoding devices shade off into general types of instruments or machines that transform one kind of energy into another. Musical instruments and printing presses, for example, are not so strictly communications devices as tape recorders or typewriters. All general types of energy transformers have special educational value, not only because of their general usefulness in facilitating communication, but also because they reveal some important features of the world: clocks, for example, reveal the relationship between motion and time, motors between motion and electricity, telescopes between distance and size. Names for relationships of this kind—but not confined to the world of physical science—make up much of the basic vocabulary of educated men.

Tools, instruments, and machines are less available now to most of the people of technological societies than they used to be. Specialized large-scale production removes them from the common scene. Artisans and mechanics can still be found in South America, Asia, and Africa, but in Europe and North America they are disappearing rapidly from public view. Not only children, but also neighbors, friends, clients, and passersby are deprived of access to firsthand demonstrations and opportunities to experiment with tools and to see the insides of the gadgets that now come out of factories encased in shiny shells. Worse than this, many modern devices can no longer be taken apart without destroying them. They are made not to be repaired but to be replaced. As a result, modern man is becoming richer in devices and poorer in his understanding of them.[1] The multiplication of product shells and factory walls, behind which tools, instruments, and machines are hidden, has the same effect educationally as the hiding of records behind the veils of national security and corporate privilege. The result is to deny people the information they need to act intelligently in their own interests. The reasons behind all this secrecy are also the same, even though the conscious motives may be different. Manufacturers guard their equipment and their products from the eyes of their customers, perhaps not consciously to keep them ignorant, but certainly in order to maintain an advantage in which ignorance is a critical factor.

Secrecy is by no means confined to capitalist countries. Professionals, managers, and specialized workers guard their privileges as jealously as owners. The techniques of modern production play into their hands equally well and are indeed partly responsible quite apart from any conscious motivation. Large-scale production has, in and of itself, profoundly anti-educational implications, as Jane Jacobs points out in her *Economy of Cities*.[2]

So long as large-scale production continues to monopolize tools, instruments, machines, and other products that have special educational value, it will be necessary to include such products in educational directories and to arrange for general access to them. Vocational schools are one attempt to supply this access, but they are far more expensive and much less educational than junk yards. Vocational schools can never serve the needs of the entire population, while junk yards could, although today junk yards are in some respects more difficult of access.

Toys and games are a special class of objects with great potential for offsetting the educational disadvantages of a technological society. They can simulate many real objects and situations, sometimes to advantage and sometimes not. Traffic rules in the classroom, for example, may be a dangerously safe simulation of a truly dangerous situation. But simple toys and games, made easily and widely accessible, could provide skill, practice, and intellectual insights with an effectiveness and economy not easy to match. Games have three great educational assets: First, they are a pleasant way of learning many skills, the practice of which might otherwise be onerous. Second, they provide a means of organizing activities among peers that make minimum demands upon leadership or authority. Finally, they are paradigms of intellectual systems, being based on elements, operations, and rules, just as mathematical systems and other intellectual models are. People familiar with games can easily be introduced to a basic understanding of the most important models of science and mathematics. Games are, of course, open to the objection of stressing scientific and technological outlooks over those of nature and the humanities. Games are also open to the objection of pitting persons against each other and of producing losers and winners. It is doubtful, however, whether competition can or should be organized out of life. Games can be so organized as to equalize advantages and thus the pleasures of winning. While everyone still knows who is best, it is usually rather difficult for one person to be best at everything.

Organizing access to toys and games falls largely into the ambit of libraries. Physical sports constitute an important exception, with problems similar to those involved where access to nature and natural things are involved.

Nature is not only becoming more distant, it is also being increasingly denatured, by exploitation and pollution on the one hand and by the sterilization of adventure on the other. The exploitation and pollution of the natural environment have been well publicized, and in terms of man's continued enjoyment of nature are of great importance. Educationally, however, cleaning up the environment may be worse than getting it dirty. Protecting children from dirt, animals, birth, sickness, death, and other natural things distorts their sense of what is real and natural. For the typical city child, nature is man-made, like everything else. Even as an adult, he has decreasing opportunities to discover the truth. Jet planes and highways keep nature at a distance, and even after he gets there, modern man's dude ranch and stage-managed safari will do little to penetrate his urban aplomb. Only a few rivers, forests, and mountain ranges remain unspoiled, and these are being invaded. Nature can no longer be left to herself, but has to be protected by man against man. Educational access complicates the problem of conservation, but education should be the main function of nature in the life of man. If proper boundaries are established between man and nature, and if his weapons are removed before he enters her, nature can continue to be man's mentor. For many people, a new guide will have to be written and new kinds of encounters devised. It is surprising and hopeful, however, to see what small enclaves of nature, truly protected, turn out to be viable.

Access to records, tools, machines, games, natural preserves, and other extraordinarily useful educational objects is relatively easy to organize. Logical classifications already exist. Directories can easily be developed; storage in libraries and arrangements for other kinds of access can be made without major difficulty. But this leaves the whole rest of the world, not as concentratedly educational perhaps, but outweighing in its total educational value all the special kinds of objects put together. The barriers to this world of ordinary objects are of several kinds. One is characterized by the automobile. Cities and many rural areas have become so unsafe for pedestrians, especially for children, that streets and roads —the physical paths to the world—are off limits to many of the world's inhabitants. If streets could again be opened to pedestrians, the city itself could again become a network of educational objects, the natural school that it has been throughout history. A second barrier, however, would still lie between the customers' area of the various shops, and the workrooms where most of the really educational objects and processes are shut away. In older cities these barriers do not exist. The tradesman works where he sells, open to public view. In the modern city, however, there is yet a third line of defense: Many machines and processes are not there at all but hidden outside the city or in places where only the persons who already know can find them. Directories that will locate this world for people who want to learn about it are indispensable, but even directories may not be easy to prepare, and access will be still more difficult to arrange. For these most interesting objects are also the most carefully guarded—the scientific, military, economic, and political objects hidden in laboratories, banks, and governmental archives.

Secrets seem natural and inevitable in the world to which we are accustomed, but the cost of keeping them is very great. Science, for example, used to be a network of people working all over the world and exchanging information freely. One of the original premises of science, which has never been repealed, was that progress depends precisely upon the open sharing of the results of scientific work. Now the members as well as the artifacts of the scientific community have been locked into national and corporate prisons, impoverishing even the citizens of these nations and the stockholders of these corporations. The special privileges they gain are more than offset by the barriers to the growth of knowledge. In a world controlled and owned by nations and corporations, only limited access to educational objects will ever be possible. Increased access to those objects that can be shared, however, may increase men's insight enough to enable them to break through these ultimate educational barriers.

9. NETWORKS OF PEOPLE

Learning is but an adjunct to ourself,
And where we are our learning likewise is.

William Shakespeare

Although people could learn much more than they do now in a world where things were freely accessible to them, it would still be helpful to have the assistance of other people. Each person might eventually learn to type, given a typewriter, but each might learn to type in a different way. Having a typist who could demonstrate the skill would help to avoid this, especially if more than one learner took advantage of the same model. If that happened, those two could compare notes and thus learn something from each other. If, finally, there were, in addition to the skill model and the two learners, someone who had taught typing before, compared the progress of various learners, and drawn some valid conclusions, this person might also be useful in reducing the time required to learn to type.

The indispensable resource for learning to type is, of course, some model of the typewriter itself. The skill model, while not indispensable, might nevertheless reduce the learning time by quite a bit, and improve the final product as well. The fellow learner, the peer, is also important, especially in providing motivation to learn and the opportunity for practice. Less important than the others is the typing teacher.

Schools reverse this kind of logic. They do not, it is true, try to teach typing without a typewriter, but they frequently try to teach foreign languages without the help of anyone who can speak them, without anyone to speak to in them, and without anything to say in them that could not just as well be said in the native language of the learner. Geography is similarly taught, without benefit of people or things from the places in question. Music is taught without instruments or musicians, science and mathematics by people who do not know them. Schools assume that the indispensable resource for learning is the teacher. Ideally this teacher should have the essential equipment for the practice of the skill and should also be able to demonstrate the skill, but these are secondary considerations. The need for learning peers is given lip service, but little use is made of peers in the learning process.

Schools are not just willfully perverse. Learning a skill, learning to practice it with someone else who is learning it, and learning how others have learned it are three different things, sometimes related but also frequently not. Schools try to find teachers who combine all three kinds of learning, but understandably they often fail. The combination is much scarcer than its elements. When they do succeed in finding the scarce combination, schools use it as if it were not scarce at all. The experienced teacher is required to act as skill model and as practice partner for individual students, to say nothing of the many duties that are unrelated to learning or teaching. The scarcest skill of the teacher is usually the ability to diagnose learning difficulties, a skill acquired by observation of learning under various circumstances. In school, the use of this scarce skill must share time with all the other functions built into the teacher's role. Most unions and school administrators oppose even specialized roles for veteran teachers who have acquired diagnostic skills. This is how schools succeed in taking plentiful learning resources and making them scarce. They package them all together, then stand the package on its head.

What schools do, nevertheless, provides an excellent model for the organization of educational resources. The model has merely to be used in reverse. Educational resources must be administered independently of each other and given priority in reverse order to that of the school: First attention must be given to the availability of information in the form of records, the instruments that produce and interpret these records, and other objects in which information is stored. Second priority must be given to the availability of skill models, people who can demonstrate the skill to be acquired. Third priority must go to the availability of real peers, fellow learners with whom learning can actually be shared. Fourth and last priority must go to the provision of educators who by virtue of experience can facilitate the use of the more essential learning resources. It might appear that educators are of first importance, if only to see that the other resources are properly valued and used. It is evident, however, that this is what educators, when incorporated into schools, do worst, not because they are educators, but because schools give them powers that corrupt their judgment.

Skill models are different from educational objects in two important respects: First, they must personally consent to their use as educational resources. Second, they frequently have enough additional flexibility and other secondary advantages to make it worth the trouble to gain this consent. In this technical age they are not strictly necessary, since their skills can all be demonstrated on records of one kind or another, but they are convenient. The superior flexibility of human models was recently demonstrated in Patrick Suppe's experiment in computerized instruction at Stanford University.[1] The computers were programmed to teach reading and numbers to beginning first-graders. The computers worked well—so long as one teacher stood behind each child to deal with his unexpected responses. Typical of these was the insertion of a pencil under the keys that operated the computer. The computer could, of course, be reprogrammed to deal with each one of these unanticipated reactions, but at the end of the third year of the experiment the programmers were lagging further behind the children than at the beginning. Computers may be able to teach other computers, but it appears that human learners may, for a time at least, continue to be better served by human models.

Skill models are in plentiful supply. There are almost always more people in any vicinity who possess a particular skill than there are people who want to learn it. The major exceptions occur when a new skill is invented or imported into a new territory. When this happens, skill models proliferate rapidly and are soon in balance with the demand for their services. Only schools and similar monopolistic institutions make skill models scarce. Schools try to forbid the use of models who have not joined the teachers' union. Some of the most famous musicians in the world, who fled from Germany at the time of the Nazi terror, were not allowed to teach music in the schools of the United States. Unions and professional associations also restrict the unauthorized use of skills, frequently creating serious shortages of vital services. Nurses, for example, are scarce in the United States primarily because the training curriculum has been extended again and again by schools of nursing, placing the cost of training beyond the means of the girls for whom the profession offers opportunities for social mobility. Restrictions on the practice of a skill are usually justified in terms of professional standards and protection of the public. Sometimes these claims are true, but more often they are patently false. The best skill models are frequently those who have just learned a skill. Children learn to read from older siblings, sometimes with ridiculous ease. English schools were really economical for a time, when Joseph Lancaster introduced the systematic use of older students to teach younger ones. This system worked better than schools usually do and was very much cheaper. It shares with other forms of schooling the fatal flaw of not allowing the learner to choose his model, his subject matter, and his place and time of instruction.[2]

Access to skill models should be organized so as to give each learner the widest choice of models and each model the greatest latitude in accepting or rejecting learners. This requires, first, an absence of restrictions and, second, a directory of skill models of all kinds. There should be no special restrictions. Model/pupil relationships are subject to risk and abuse, as is any kind of human relationship, but the general laws and customs that cover all such relationships provide the best available protection. Learning in and of itself creates no additional hazards. The advantage of permitting the learner to seek and find a model from whom he will learn is, in general, worth all the additional risk that such latitude entails. Not learning what needs to be learned is likely to involve the greatest risks of all.

Developing directories of skill models is not intrinsically difficult. Truly convenient and comprehensive directories might be so valuable, however, as to warrant considerable investment. Responsibility for developing and administering such directories should probably be vested in a public utility. Skill models willing to offer evidence of their skills might be offered free registration. Those who chose not to do this could, nevertheless, retain the freedom to make such arrangements as were possible using their own means of publicity.

Having learned a skill, people need someone with whom to practice. But peers are important even before practice. Who would bother to learn a skill unless there were others with whom to share it, fellow explorers of the new ground opened by the skill? Many skills are learned primarily with peers, taking advantage of the skill models in the general environment. Often, peers and skill models are hard to distinguish. In ordinary interpersonal relations there is neither need nor advantage in distinguishing skill models from peers. On the contrary, learning occurs best when such distinctions are not made. There is, however, an important distinction that can be ignored only if the individuals involved are willing to ignore it. Peers are by definition equals, deriving mutual benefits from their relationship. They can play tennis together, go exploring together, study mathematics together, or build a camp together. If they are peers, they contribute more or less equally to each other's objectives. Helping a smaller brother or sister learn what he wants to learn is different. It may be equally enjoyable for a while, but the enjoyment palls more quickly. Peer relationships are freely chosen, freely kept. Skill-modeling frequently requires some sort of compensation for the model if the relationship is maintained as long as the learner would like. A method for compensating skill models is therefore needed, although it is not needed in relationships of peers.

Finding peers is merely a matter of knowing where they are and being able to get there, write, or call on the telephone. Neighborhoods free of major hazards are all that most children need for the purpose. As skills develop, however, the better ballplayers go farther afield to find worthy competitors, the botany bug outgrows his neighborhood pals, the serious ballet addicts find their ranks thinning out.

Schools supplement neighborhoods, as things are now organized, but schools create as many barriers to peer groups as opportunities for them. In schools, peer groups form around the goals of teachers or around the interests of dope pushers. Student-initiated groups concerned with education have a hard time competing with either. But, for teen-agers, the neighborhood no longer serves as an adequate base for contacts. If it did, the telephone and the automobile would be more readily dispensable.

For adults, with their frequently highly specialized interests, even the largest cities cannot always provide true peers. The best illustration of this is the scientific community, which must be world-wide for the most fruitful peer encounters to occur. The scientific community also illustrates how peer matches can be fostered or frustrated.

The logical structure of science provides a framework for identifying persons of similar interests. Its journals provide means of communication. Its rules of logic and criteria of evidence provide the parameters for fruitful encounters. Its achievements unfailingly generate new problems, which beckon explorers with common interests. All these advantages of science as a network of related interests that provide an ideal basis for peer-group formation, have now been offset by institutional barriers. National and corporate interests now dictate who may speak or write to whom, in what terms, when, how, and where. Only the model of a scientific community is left, available for other interest groups that have been less successful in forming fruitful peer groups than scientists used to be.

The advantages of science in fostering communication among peers are no more natural than the forces that have now disrupted them. The modern "logical" structure of science did not exist a century ago. Neither did its current journals, nor its present rules of logic or standards of evidence. The beginnings were already there, but, two centuries ago, even those were only dim foreshadowings.

Fortunately, other communities of interest do not have to retrace the steps of science. The example and the products of science make it possible to short-cut these steps. Today any area of interest can be so described that a computer can match the persons who share it. Learners in search of peers need only identify themselves and their interests in order to find matches in the neighborhood, city, nation, or world. The computer is not indispensable. In the neighborhood, a bulletin board will do; in the city, a newspaper; in the nation, a national magazine; in the world, an international journal. All these media and others are and should be used to find peer matches, but computers can make the matching easier and more flexible.

The operation of a peer-matching network would be simple. The user would identify himself by name and address and describe the activity he wanted to share. A computer would send him back the names and addresses of all who had inserted similar descriptions. People using the system would become known only to their potential peers.

Abuses of our matching systems are easy to visualize. They range from the danger of master data files compiled by government agencies for the control of citizens to the danger of sex perverts' misusing information posted on bulletin boards. As in the case of model/pupil relationships, these dangers increase as contacts increase, but they are not increased by the educational purposes of these contacts. Monitoring systems provide one type of safeguard, but also raise the question of who monitors the monitors. Providing potential users of a communications medium with ample information about the dangers of its use, and with suggestions for countering these dangers, is the best short-term safeguard. In the longer term, only progress toward a just society, which would alter people's motives toward one another, can give us a world both safe and free.

As in the case of skill models, a public utility might provide free service for the finding of peers. This would be justified not only in educational terms but also as buttressing the right of free assembly. The same right should also be extended to include prohibition of involuntary assembly, in the form of compulsory attendance at school. If freedom of the press and free assembly were taken seriously, and public means provided to make them available to everyone, compulsory school attendance, military service, and other common current compulsions would become unnecessary.

As schools are replaced by networks of educational objects, skill models, and peers, the demand for educators, rather than declining, will probably increase. These educators will perform different functions than are now performed in school, and not all of them will be the same people. The need for those with real ability in administration, teaching, and scholarship will increase, and their rewards in terms of educational achievement, professional freedom, and income will also increase. Schoolmen whose skills are primarily in the hiring, supervision, and firing of teachers; public relations with parents; curriculum making; textbook purchasing; maintenance of grounds and facilities; and the supervision of interscholastic athletic competition may not find a market for their skills. Neither will all the baby-sitting, lesson-planning, and record-keeping teachers, unless they have skills that can be turned to other uses, or unless they leave education for more honestly designated employment. This is no put-down of school teachers and school administrators as people. Schools put them in impossible positions, just as they do students.

At least three kinds of professional educators will be in strong demand: first, architects and administrators of the educational resource networks that have been briefly described; second, pedagogues who can help design effective individual educational programs, diagnose educational difficulties, and prescribe effective remedies; and third, leaders in every branch of learning.

Educational-resource networks are simple in principle and will be effective only if they are kept simple in operation. The kind of simplicity required, however, is frequently the mark of genius. People who can multiply the services available to others and still stay out of their way are relatively rare people.

The designers of the new networks will have to understand knowledge, people, and the societies they live in. They will have to be dedicated to the idea of student-directed, individualized education. They will have to understand the barriers to the flow of relevant information and how to reduce them without generating offsetting counteractions. They will, above all, have to be able to resist the eternal temptation of subtly directing the studies of their clients instead of opening ever new and possibly dangerous doors for their investigation.

Teachers were greatly honored before there were schools, and will be again when they are freed to practice their profession without the constraints of forced attendance, mandatory curriculums, and classroom walls. The core of an independent educational profession will be the pedagogue, a bad word now but one that will come into its own when students, parents, and teachers are free to make responsible educational decisions. They will find then that they need advice and assistance in selecting learning programs, choosing skill models, discovering peers, finding leadership in difficult endeavors. Unlike the network administrator, the independently practicing pedagogue will not have to suppress his opinions and values in favor of those of his client. He will be free to make value judgments, because his clients will also be free. He will have no way of shaping their decisions except through the persuasiveness of his advice. And he had better be right as well as persuasive, for his clients will hold him responsible. This profession is not for the fainthearted, but the competent pedagogue will find in it the rewards of the old family doctor, the man who made the reputation that modern medical specialists are still living on. There will, of course, be room for many pedagogic specialties, such as testing and educational psychiatry, which will be in less demand as the damage done by schools declines. Eventually the new pedagogic profession may succumb to the overspecialization that now afflicts medicine, but by that time it will have made its contribution.

The role of the educational leader is more elusive than that of the network administrator or the pedagogue. This is because leadership itself is hard to define. Walter Bagehot's description of a leader as a man out in front when people decide to go in a certain direction, has not been improved upon.[3] It takes nothing away from the leader who positions himself for relevant reasons.

Leadership, like education, is not confined to intellectual pursuits. It occurs wherever people do things together, and especially when the going gets rough. This is when true leadership distinguishes itself, usually depending more on relevant prior learning than on the personal qualities so dear to the world of fiction. There is no valid test of leadership, even past experience. As Thomas Kuhn points out in *The Structure of Scientific Revolutions,* even in fields as rigorous as physical science, the most distinguished leaders are periodically proved basically wrong.[4] There is, on the other hand, no substitute for leadership, and leaders remain one of the vital educational resources that learners must be helped to find. Leaders will, of course, recommend themselves, and this must be depended upon even in systematic attempts to match learners with leaders.

In practice, there will always be a fuzzy line between skill models and leaders. Both are specific to the content of what is being learned or done; both are subject-matter specialists. Mountaineers cannot substitute for physicists, and vice-versa. The directories and administrative means that serve to locate skill models can also be used to locate leaders, who will identify themselves by the claims they make, the terms they insist upon, and the behavior they exhibit in actual encounter. Networks can be helpful in finding potential leadership, but the true commodity will always be recognized only after the fact.

There are other kinds of human beings who can be called educational resources only by stretching the concept. These people are nevertheless more important educationally than all the resources described above. They are mothers, fathers, children, lovers, and all the other kinds of people who distinguish human beings from featherless bipeds. These people cannot be treated as educational resources, because they are primarily something else. Familial, erotic, economic, and political relationships cannot be organized as if their main purpose were educational. All, however, have enormously important educational implications, which cannot be neglected even though they cannot be manipulated for specific educational purposes. Unless people enjoy, in the main, good human relationships, they can neither be educated nor educate themselves. The most fundamental educational resource, then, is a world in which most people have good relationships with others. Perhaps paradoxically, universal education may itself be the principal means of realizing such a world.

It should be emphasized again that distinguishing the various kinds of human educational resources makes sense only in economic and administrative terms. It would be an error for individuals to treat each other or themselves as restricted to one or another of these categories. For economic reasons, however, these or similar distinctions are vital. The packaging of educational resources determines whether these resources are scarce or plentiful, expensive or cheap. And this in turn determines whether education, and all other privilege, is to remain the prerogative of the few or whether education and justice are to be made available for all.

10. FINANCING UNIVERSAL EDUCATION

The way to establish an institution is to finance it.

Justice William O. Douglas

In a just world, or in a world trying to achieve justice, public expenditures on education should be inversely proportional to the wealth of the student. Private expenditures on education are made almost entirely on behalf of the better off, so that equal total expenditures on education would require that public funds for education go in a higher proportion to the poor. Even this would not equalize educational opportunity, since the parents and the homes of the better off represent an investment in their education that needs to be offset. Finally, the poor suffer the handicap of the culture of silence, the inheritance of magic and myth designed to insure their continued docility. It is this, rather than deficient genes, that handicaps the learning of their children; this plus the punishment of failure and disapproval, which is their customary lot in schools. These disadvantages, not inherent in them and not of their own making, require additional expenditure on the education of the poor. If all the public funds allotted to education in every nation were spent exclusively upon the poor, it would still take many generations to offset the handicaps that generations of exploitation have imposed upon them.

It should be clear that even the first step in equalizing educational opportunity among social classes requires an allocation of educational resources outside the school system. The only ways of making sure that poor children get even an equal share of *public* funds for education are either to segregate them completely in schools of their own, or to give the money directly to them. The first of these alternatives has been tried and has conspicuously failed.

The United States Supreme Court's anti-segregation decision of 1954 was based squarely upon the finding that the prior, "separate but equal" doctrine had not worked. No country in the world fails to provide both more and better schooling to its more-privileged children.

Putting financial command of educational resources in the hands of learners does not solve all the problems of allocating these resources, but it is an indispensable step toward a solution. Not only the problem of equalizing opportunity across class lines but many other problems discussed above become manageable with the aid of this principle. Schools would stand, adjust, or fail according to the satisfaction of their clients. Other educational institutions would develop in accordance with their ability to satisfy client needs. Learners would choose whether to learn on the job or full-time, which skills they wanted to learn, at what age they wanted to use their educational resources, and how.

This presupposes a system of lifetime educational accounts administered in early childhood by parents, in which resource credit could be accumulated and over which the learner, from a very early age at least, would have a veto power.

In the world as seen by Adam Smith, this would solve all the problems. In the real world, there is still an imperfect distribution of the supply of the real resources required for education, and there is, furthermore, imperfect knowledge of what resources are needed and where they are to be found. This imperfect knowledge is not confined to learners. The would-be suppliers of educational resources also lack knowledge of where their potential clients are and of what they need. There is finally the age-old problem of imperfect character: people who want something for nothing and those who will sell anything to make a profit. If perfect competition and complete knowledge existed, they would offset the problem of man's venality. Since they do not, it remains to compound the evil.

A system of personal educational accounts and a system of public educational utilities, such as those suggested in the two preceding chapters, would complement each other. They could be combined in a number of ways. One way would be to make the public utilities self-supporting, as the postal system is supposed to be, charging each user for the approximate cost of the service rendered him. Another way would be to make the services of the resource networks completely free. This would require dividing public funds for education between the support of the proposed utilities and provision for the proposed personal accounts.

Besides these alternatives, various mixtures are possible: providing some services free while charging for others or charging some people and not others, according to age, income, or other criteria. The possible combinations are too numerous to permit exhaustive discussion, but a few are worth mentioning. The networks might, for example, provide a directory service free, locating skill models, objects, peers, etc., but do nothing further to economically facilitate access. This would leave it to the learner to buy or borrow the indicated book, or pay the skill model, out of his personal account. Alternatively, libraries and stores of educational objects in common demand might be maintained for the free use of the public; reading and mathematics teachers might be publicly paid to teach elementary skills.

These alternatives contemplate only the use of public funds derived from tax revenues and divided between educational-resource networks and personal educational accounts. Additional financial arrangements are conceivable. An educational bank might be established, in which educational services could be deposited and from which educational credit could be received. Skill models, for example, might elect not to be paid in cash but to accumulate credit for themselves and their children. Learners might borrow from the bank either credit with a skill model who is accumulating credit, or cash to pay one who wants cash, and the learner might later repay the bank either in cash or in service as a skill model for someone else.

An educational bank could not compete in the market with banks less restricted in their activities and in a better position to enforce the repayment of loans. Government support for such a bank, or for any free service by an educational-resource network, or even for the establishment of such a network, would constitute an educational subsidy. The use of taxes for education is, of course, already a subsidy, but if educational tax funds were diverted entirely into educational accounts,

there would be no subsidy for one kind of education over another. Today there is. Graduate schools are highly favored
over elementary levels. Science is favored over other subjects.
Nor are subsidies confined to the public sector. Monopolistic
industries are able to pass on the costs of educating both their
employees and the public, because they can set their prices
to absorb such costs. Government bureaus have even greater
latitude. The military have almost unlimited funds for training
and almost unlimited capacity to educate the public, not only
by spending money but by manipulating information. The
mass media are currently subsidized by the advertisers of
products and services, while producing corporations in turn
are able to charge the public for the education they impose
upon them. Some educational subsidies are paid directly out
of the public purse. Others are collected by private corporations under permissive public laws. All are expressions of public policy more or less openly admitted.

Educational policy would be most open to public view if
all public funds were channeled into personal educational accounts, and all educational institutions, including the proposed resource networks, had to be self-supporting. At present levels of expenditure, this would provide every man,
woman, and child in the United States with two hundred and
fifty dollars per year to spend on education. It would also
force all elementary and high schools, universities and graduate schools to charge tuition high enough to pay all costs.
At first sight, many a scholastic career would appear to be
nipped in the bud. But each newborn child would have a lifetime fund of seventeen thousand dollars to finance his personal education. Each twenty-year-old could count on twelve
thousand dollars, each forty-year-old on seven thousand dollars, each sixty-year-old on two thousand dollars. This is the
average amount of schooling the American public is buying
now, through taxes, for each of its citizens.[1] It is roughly
equivalent to a college education. The fact that so few people
get it merely underscores the inequality of the present distribution. Actually, few of those who now receive more would
be seriously hurt if public funds were divided equally. All

but a few would be able to finance their additional education privately. Poor children, on the other hand, would have five times as much educational support as they now receive. On the average, these poor children would get the same amount they now get up to age fifteen. They would then, however, still have four times as much left. Many poor children become able to profit from formal training only at about this age, although this may be only because the present system of schooling is so poorly adapted to their needs.

What about those who, today, spend at a much faster rate? Would the average middle-class child who now uses up his quota of public funds by about age twenty-one be retarded by having to keep within his annual quota? Under at least three circumstances he would not: First, his family might supplement his allowance. Current private investment in education in the United States is only one fourth of public expenditure, one fifth of the total. Second, he might not attend schools but get his education elsewhere at lower cost. Third, he might borrow against his lifetime allowance. Under favorable circumstances this would appear to be relatively safe. If the student's family were fairly well off but reluctant to invest their own money, they could probably, in one way or another, insure against the risk of failure. If, on the other hand, the family were poor but the student able and promising for his chosen career, insurance might be bought at public expense to cover his risk.

What about people who didn't use their allowance? The taxpayers might be allowed to benefit. Allowances might be increased in subsequent years. Families might be permitted to pool their allowances. Adults would probably learn fairly quickly to use what they had coming, and this could work to the great benefit of education, the adults themselves, and their society. Adults acting on their own behalf would be shrewd buyers of education. Their demand would bring educational resources into the market that younger people would also use, once the demonstration had been made. Many now-passive middle-aged and older people would come alive and begin to take a more-informed interest in their own and in public affairs.

How would educational allowances actually be spent? What would happen to schools? How would profiteering be controlled? Answers depend very much on development of the resource networks previously described. Capital investment in these networks would have to have a prior claim on public funds for education, even if this investment were to be repaid by the fees charged for service. If these networks were well designed and operated, they would influence the investments of many learners, especially adults at first. Many of these adults would be parents, however, whose children would also soon begin to use the networks.

Schools would, for a time, continue to be used by parents dependent on the custodial care they offered and by students far enough along to be dependent upon them. Schools could not, however, continue to function at the level of today, since the public funds available to the age group they serve would be less than one third of the public funds that schools receive now. A few schools might survive—old, established private schools and a few public schools in rich suburbs whose patrons could afford to keep them up and could also afford not to worry too much about the economic future of their children. Most people would soon discover more-efficient ways of learning and more-pleasant ways of spending time than in school.

Charlatans and profiteers might have a field day for a time. But, if the networks functioned properly, they would soon be checked, not by suppression primarily, but by the competition of honest suppliers and skill models, aided by competent pedagogues advising parents and students. Controls of the type offered by better-business bureaus would be sufficient, too inefficient to do much harm, but available for use against a real mountebank.

The money that is now so insufficient for schools would be more than enough to support an enormous network of educational objects and to partially support a number of skill models, pedagogues, and educational leaders far in excess of the number of teachers employed today. Many would work only part time as skill models and educational leaders, practicing their skills and pursuing their explorations for other purposes as well. Educational counselors working full time could serve a clientele of a thousand persons, giving each on the average a couple of hours per year.

Financial magic? Not at all. The cost of custodial care would in large part be transferred back from the public to the private purse. Most of it is now provided for people too old to need it—old enough to work and, in many cases, better off working.

While no financial magic is involved, two major social problems would obviously increase if schools were disestablished. Younger children would have to be cared for, while older ones would have to find employment. Some older children could be employed in the care of the younger. Some, not suitable as caretakers, would nevertheless be excellent models of athletic, musical, and many other skills that younger children really want to learn. Still others could build playgrounds, not once for all, but day by day, in streets and vacant lots and fields and forests; places that can be made at least temporarily safe for younger children through the efforts of older ones.

Not all older children, of course, should be employed in looking after youngsters. Some should help their elders or even substitute for them part time, freeing some of them—the ones with appropriate interests and talents—to spend time with the younger children or to direct the activities of the teen-agers. While teen-agers should work, they should not be confined to routine work. An enormous number of ecological and social research projects could be carried out by young people. An equal variety of artistic projects, from painting the town to the production of plays and festivals, could not only engage the young but benefit the old.

The core of all these projects, the principle underlying the work of older children and the care of younger ones, should be the creation—or re-creation—of the good life. There is not really so much difference of opinion about what that is, especially where children are involved. The problems, rather, are those of overcoming barriers, finding staff, financing. But the disestablishment of schools would release a lot of money and a lot of talent.

Starting from where we are, how could this money and talent be redirected? Under the principles proposed above, public funds for education would be redirected from schools to students, teachers, taxpayers, or businessmen.

Educational accounts would channel funds that now go directly to schools through the hands of students. Students might still spend them on schools, either because the law gave them no option or because the schools succeeded in hoodwinking them or because the schools, under the impact of necessity, succeeded in providing what people wanted. In all probability, schools would get a steadily declining share of the educational dollar if it went directly to students.

Students would probably elect to spend some of their dollars directly on teachers, by-passing the schools, but there are also other ways in which teachers could profit at the expense of schools. Any significant weakening in the regulatory power of schools would tend to have this effect; their power to compel attendance, for example, or to certify compliance with curriculum requirements. If students were to receive credit by examination without attending classes, teachers would be in increased demand as tutors. For them to increase their earnings would, of course, require a transfer of the savings resulting from reduced school attendance to a tutorial account. Most school laws would not have to be changed to make this possible.

One way of transferring funds from schools to taxpayers is merely to reduce the resources earmarked for education. Another way, however, is to shift educational emphasis from children to adults. Since there are more taxpayers than parents, education distributed over the adult population would tend to match educational benefits with tax liability. The taxpayer, of course, would get back a dollar earmarked for education in place of one that had no strings attached, but this might have good educational by-products. The taxpayer would insist upon maximum control of his dollar and would spend it on education valued by him rather than dictated by another.

There are several ways to shift the educational dollar from schools to businessmen. Educational accounts are one. Performance contracts are another. Such contracts have recently been written by a number of schools with enterprisers who guarantee to teach a testable skill and who are not paid unless they do. Still another way to benefit business is to shift the burden of teaching from people to reproducible objects, be these books or computers.

There is an understandable reluctance on the part of educational liberals to make common cause with taxpayers and businessmen. Some academicians claim, for example, that mass media, especially television, already have more educational influence than schools, and that weakening the schools would merely strengthen the hold of business interests on the minds of men, women, and children. Galbraith even argues that the academic community is one of our main hopes of escaping the worst implications of the new industrial state. The evidence does not support him. There is no major issue—war, pollution, exploitation, racism—on which the academic community, as such, has a discernible stand. There are intelligent, courageous men in schools and universities, as there are elsewhere, but they receive no effective support from their institutions. In the exceptional case, in which an institution has shielded an unpopular dissident, it has also muffled his voice. The worst causes, on the other hand, have had no difficulty in recruiting academics to their support while institutions of learning have entered into contracts with all kinds of other institutions for all kinds of purposes.

But this does not meet the argument that jumping out of the school fat might land us in the television fire. If one believes in people and in freedom, this would still be a step forward. No one is compelled to watch television and everyone knows who is talking and why. People learn, if they are given a chance, although not always what we want them to learn. God had to gamble on people and has frequently lost. Without this gamble, however, there would be no humanity.

If educational liberals are unwilling to co-operate with tax-payers and businessmen, they must submit to an ever-waxing educational bureaucracy whose efficiency is steadily declining. If, on the other hand, real education were to result from this proposed unholy alliance, this would in itself reduce the danger of economic domination. Responsibility is best divided between private and public interests if policy is made by those who do not stand to gain by its implementation and carried out by those who do. Taxpayers, businessmen, and educational liberals can be satisfactory allies if none are permitted to write the rules under which all will operate.

It would be a mistake, however, to conclude that a competitive market in educational resources would necessarily result in good education. If everyone were already educated it might, but this is to assume the end we are seeking. Starting from where we are, certain educational institutions would have to be subsidized.

One of the most important tasks would be to induce parents and employers to reassume their proper educational responsibilities. Every thinking person knows that real education occurs primarily at home and at work, but a number of facts have conspired to rob this truth of its former general acceptance. The modern organization of society, by offering free schooling, rewards both parents and employers, in the short run, for reducing their normal educational roles. In addition, schools benefit politically potent parents, while business gains from any reduction in production costs. Similarly, the competitive consumption in which modern households engage induces them to save on costs for which there is nothing to display. Except perhaps in certain academic households, bright children are harder to show off than shiny automobiles.

This kind of dominantly economic competition among producers and households is itself the product of a particular kind of legal structure. Until this is changed, some kind of subsidy will be needed to put educational processes back where they occur most rationally and economically—in the home and on the job.

Another place where a great deal of effective education

used to occur was in the practice of the arts. Before modern technology took over, all production involved the practice of art. What we now call the fine arts were integrated with the practice of other crafts, and people learned not only by working with more-experienced masters but also from associates practicing related arts. In the early stages of industrialization, now rapidly passing, this kind of learning was disrupted. It could now be re-established, since the demand for industrial labor is rapidly declining, but only if people who learn, teach, and practice the various arts are given a dependable claim on the goods and services produced by modern technology. Unrestricted competition between men and machines is not a natural phenomenon, but one that has been deliberately engineered in modern societies. Most countries of the world are frustrated in their efforts to bring this competition about. Modern countries may find it no less difficult to undo, but they must undo it if the arts are to reclaim an educational role that can in no other way be performed. There is no comparable way of teaching everyone the essential skills of hand and foot, ear and eye, mind and tongue.

In addition to the revival of traditional educational institutions, the modern world requires the new ones, which have been described as networks, or directories of educational objects, skill models, learning peers, or professional educators. Public utilities charged with administering educational networks could be self-supporting, once established, and might even be established with minimum public investment, but some experimental operation and testing would probably have to be publicly subsidized.

Schools cannot be disestablished and education made available to all while the rest of the world remains unchanged. Competition among nations, classes, and individuals will have to be replaced by co-operation. This means placing limits upon what any individual or group can consume, produce, or do to others—limits that are being widely transgressed today by many individuals and groups. Acceptance of such limits implies an increased self-insight into what the real interests and possibilities of groups and individuals are. More than that, it implies a sacrifice of short-term interests for those which are more enduring. This is not the kind of behavior for which the human race is noted. It remains quite probable, therefore, that it will not be learned except under the impact of catastrophe. There is no need, however, to plan for catastrophe, while there is every need to plan for its avoidance.

11. THE REVOLUTIONARY ROLE OF EDUCATION

Men had better be without education than be educated by their rulers; for this education is but the mere breaking in of the steer to the yoke; the mere discipline of the hunting dog, which by dint of severity is made to forego the strongest impulse of his nature, and instead of devouring his prey, to hasten with it to the feet of his master.

Thomas Hodgkins, 1823.

Effective alternatives to schools cannot occur without other widespread changes in society. But there is no point in waiting for other changes to bring about a change in education. Unless educational alternatives are planned and pursued, there is no assurance they will occur, no matter what else happens. If they do not, the other changes are likely to be superficial and short-lived. Educational change, on the other hand, will bring other fundamental social changes in its wake.

True education is a basic social force. Present social structures could not survive an educated population even if only a substantial minority were educated. Something more than schooling is obviously in question here. People are schooled to accept a society. They are educated to create or re-create one.

Education has the meaning here that deep students of education and of human nature have always given it. None has defined it better than Paulo Freire, the Brazilian educator, who describes it as becoming critically aware of one's reality in a manner that leads to effective action upon it.[1] An educated man understands his world well enough to deal with it effectively. Such men, if they existed in sufficient numbers, would not leave the absurdities of the present world unchanged.

Some such men do exist—men who understand reality well enough to deal with it effectively. Today they exist in small numbers, most of them engaged in running the world for their own convenience. If, in any society, the proportion of persons so educated were twenty percent instead of two, or thirty instead of three, such a society could no longer be run by a few for their own purposes, but would have to be run for the general welfare. The laurels of leadership lose their appeal if spread over more than a few. Whenever, as in Pilgrim New England, ancient Athens, or early Rome, a reasonable proportion of the population have been educated, in the sense of understanding their reality well enough to act effectively upon it, their societies have been truly democratic.

Nation-states as they exist today could not for long survive an educated population. Nations made up of educated citizens would tend to merge with other nations. This could, of course, begin to happen within the nominal framework of the nation-state. Geographical boundaries would not have to change. When immigration and tariff restrictions change sufficiently, political frontiers become meaningless.

Class distinctions would also tend to disappear in educated societies, as indeed they have tended to do in certain periods of history. This does not mean that individual differences of value-position or privilege would disappear. In a changing society, new differences would occur as rapidly as old ones were equalized. It would be difficult, however, to identify differences resulting from constant mobility with either class, race, or any other socially identifying label. An educated society would become and remain highly pluralistic, with many loosely related, fluid hierarchies based on a large number of independent value criteria. Some people might be rich, some powerful, others popular, still others loved or respected or strong, but not very many could be all of these for very long.

An educated population would make not only their nations but also their specialized institutions responsive to the needs and desires of clients and workers, in addition to those of managers. Any sizable educated minority would never put up with inadequate health and education services, environmental pollution, political policy control by military-industrial cliques, or advertiser control of mass media, to say nothing of traffic jams, slums, and the host of other absurdities that afflict modern societies.

No educational magic is implied. Not even educated people could solve these problems in their present context. What they could and would do is recognize an impossible context and change it. They would realize, for example, that competitive consumption is an impossible way of life for more than short periods or small minorities. Once this were grasped, much of our present production and employment would be seen as not only unnecessary but actually harmful. War materials are an obvious case, but schooling, pretentious short-lived consumer durables, advertising, corporate and governmental junketing, and a host of other products and activities are scarcely less so.

One difficulty in doing anything about these matters is that the present way of life of so many privileged people depends upon keeping things as they are. Education alone cannot solve this problem. It can help people see what shifting sand their present security rests upon. It can help them visualize feasible alternatives, although something more may be required to realize them. This is merely to say that education alone cannot bring about revolutionary social change. It can go much further, however, than people who confuse education with schooling are accustomed to think.

The world of schools conceives the problem of education as one of inducing students to learn what they are supposed to know. From this point of view, it seems nonsensical to think of people as being blocked from knowing and learning. Yet clearly they are. Most of the people of the world sweat their lives out on land that belongs to others, constantly in debt to their landlords, with no control over the prices of what they buy or sell, helpless in their misery and kept helpless not only by denial of information and opportunity to learn but by deliberate distortion of the facts of their lives. Witch doctors, priests, politicians, and purveyors of profitable nostrums vie with each other to keep these people sunk in their ignorance and unaware of their true condition. They are aided in these attempts by the physical misery in which their victims are forced to live, misery so great and so hopeless that it must somehow be justified, somehow disguised, in order to make it bearable.

Education for these people does not consist primarily in learning to read, but in learning to understand and do something about their miserable situation. This may involve learning to read, but it must obviously include other things, without which the ability to read would not be of any real value. Suppose that a few children in such an environment do learn to read and thus escape. This does nothing to help those who stay behind to breed more children.

Much of what people in this situation need to know, in order to basically improve their lot, is actively withheld or hidden from them. Paulo Freire found in working with Brazilian peasants that they immediately learned to read words with real meaning in their actual situation.[1] But Freire's clients had no sooner learned to read than they organized peasant leagues through which they tried to bargain with their employers. Although they were scrupulously careful to observe the law and the customs of the region, their employers, government authorities, and the Church united against them. Their leaders were fired and jailed, while the Church denied its sacraments to members of the league until Protestant missionaries began to make converts among them.

Freire calls the rural culture of Latin America a culture of silence. By this he means that the rural masses, having been deprived of any real voice in the matters that concern them most, have forgotten how to speak or even to think about these matters except in terms of the rationalizing mythologies supplied by their superiors. In Freire's terms, they have lost the "word." The term is used here as it is in the first verse of the Gospel according to St. John: "In the beginning was the word and the word was with God and the word was God." What the members of the culture of silence have lost is their God-given birthright of naming—and thus understanding and controlling—their world. To understand how the word might be lost to a whole class of men, it is necessary only to remember the origins of this class in the institution of slavery. Slaves were allowed to sing, to chant, to chatter, and to gossip, but they were not allowed to say anything serious about their own condition or about the society that kept them in this condition. For generations, the children of slaves were raised without reference to such matters, and even with conscious repression, by parents, of references that innocent children might make. It is easy to see how the word was lost to slaves and their successors.

The current practice of religion as it affects the peasants and urban workers of Latin America illustrates very aptly how the word remains lost to these populations. In the rural areas, this religion is Catholicism, but in many regions it is Catholicism in name only. Actually it is often merely an overlay of popular saint culture upon a base of indigenous witchcraft, the content of the Catholic and witchcraft elements of the amalgam varying from one region to another.[2] The social functions performed by these amalgams are the same, however, with no discernible differences in efficacy. They all effect cures, control anti-social impulses or re-establish order when the controls fail, and provide a structure of meaning for celebration of birth, death, marriage, and other critical events in the lives of individuals. More important from a social point of view, they legitimize ownership of the land by the rich, condone and justify the privileges enjoyed by the elites at the expense of the poor, and exalt the charitable acts of the elite and their symbolic roles in religious, political, economic, and familial affairs. They provide the peasants with a set of after-life rewards to console them for their misery in the present life and represent their current sufferings as the will of God and acquiescence in these sufferings as the height of virtue.

There are, of course, many Catholic priests in Latin America whose behavior contradicts every line of the above description, who castigate the rich and assist, arouse, and lead the peasants in their search for justice. These priests are sometimes killed, more often locked up as mad, and still more often assigned to innocuous duties or dismissed. Occasionally their work is welcomed and supported by bishops who agree with them.

When Latin American peasants move to the cities and become urban workers, they are converted in large numbers to a variety of fundamentalist Protestant sects. Even Catholic employers frequently prefer these converts as workers and hire them selectively. They are likely to be more sober, more faithful to their wives and families, and more earnest about their work, about keeping their children in school, about acquiring possessions, and about getting ahead in the world.

Their behavior supports perfectly Weber's hypothesis on the relationship between Protestantism and industrialization. The personally permissive nominal Catholicism—so perfectly adjusted to rural Latin America and so sharply in contrast with its counterparts in rural Ireland and northern Spain—is poorly suited to São Paulo, Buenos Aires, Mexico City, and the lesser industrial centers of Latin America. So is the more-sophisticated urban Catholicism of Latin American cities, with its emphasis on the rights of labor, the obligations of the employer, and, in general, on social justice in the modern industrial world. The teachings of some of the older Protestant sects are no more in the interests of urban employers than modern Catholicism, and these sects make fewer converts among the workers.

It may seem odd that workers join the sects whose teachings are in their employers' interest rather than their own. This is only partly because employers select as workers the members of these sects. It is also because relatively powerless workers psychologically need a religion that will reconcile the contradictions between their employers' interests and their own.

We take as great pains to hide the facts of life from our children as the Brazilian landlords and urban employers do to hide them from their peasants and workers. Like them, we not only hide and distort facts but invoke the assistance of great institutions and elaborate mythologies. Facts of life are not confined to sex; about this we are becoming less inhibited even with children. But relative incomes of families on the block, the neighborhood power structure, why father didn't get his promotion or mother her chairmanship, why Jimmy is smoking pot or Susie is having an out-of-town vacation: these things, which children perversely want to know, are obviously not for them. Neither is ballet at the expense of reading, karate in place of math, or the anatomy of flies as a substitute for botany out of a book. Schools are obviously as much designed to keep children from learning what really intrigues them as to teach them what they ought to know. As a result, most children learn to read and do not read, learn their num-

bers and hate mathematics, shut themselves off in classrooms
and do their learning in cloakrooms, hangouts, and on the
road.

We ourselves are no better off than our children. Attempts
to get the contents of cans and boxes clearly labeled are
treated as attacks on private enterprise. Any real probing of
foreign policy is labeled subversive, while the basic facts are
hidden behind the screen of national security. The enemies
of every military power in the world know more about its
military capacities and intentions than is available to the makers of its own laws. Spies, bellhops, charwomen, valets, and
ladies' maids are the privileged exceptions to the conspiracy
of secrecy in which we live.

There are, of course, the best of reasons for all the secrecy
and mystification. Children might be permanently scarred by
premature exposure to death, suffering, sex, or the sordid facts
of economic and political life. Mechanics might be embar-
rassed if car owners were given detailed descriptions of their
own motorcars. A little knowledge is dangerous, not only for
laymen, but for their doctors, lawyers, and accountants. If customers were allowed to know what they are buying, competitors could also find it out. If national security barriers were
lowered, the enemy would learn even more at lower cost.
These reasons range from valid to ludicrous, but even the
valid ones are valid only in the context of the society in which
we live. In this society, Paulo Freire is a threat and so is
the free education of our children and of ourselves. At present,
this education is not free. People are systematically prevented
from learning those things which are most important for them
to know. They are deliberately misled by institutional distor-
tions of facts and by the propagation of religious, political,
and economic mythologies that make it extraordinarily difficult to get a clear glimpse of relevant truth. Protestants see
clearly through the Catholic smoke screen. Capitalists have
no difficulty in seeing how the communists brainwash their
victims. Englishmen and Frenchmen see through each other's machinations without the slightest trouble. Only our own
camouflage confuses us.

The secular significance of the great religious teachers of the past can be seen in the important role of disclosure in true education. Apart from the transcendental content of their teaching, Moses, Jesus, Mohammed, Gautama, Lao-tse—to mention only a few of the most famous—disclosed major truths to millions of people. Each of their teachings was, of course, subsequently used to obscure the very enlightenment they brought, to justify what they denounced, and to convict those whom they justified. Nevertheless, the truths they revealed could never again be totally hidden. Today's injustice stands convicted by their teachings, and today's ideals are built upon them. Their teachings were not esoteric. Many of their contemporaries must have seen what they saw, felt what they felt, but lacked the security to trust their judgment, the courage to speak their minds, or the charisma to attract disciples.

In our time, the great teachers have spoken in secular terms. Marx, Freud, Darwin, to again name only the most famous, have revealed to millions truths that many others sensed but could not equally well express. Thanks in part to the great teachers of the past, today's significant truths lie closer to the surface. They are there for many to see. The veneer that covers them is frequently transparent; the hypocrisy with which they are disguised is often so blatant as to be insulting. Today no genius is required to discover, reveal, and proclaim the truths that could set men free. But it still takes doing. This is the role of the true teacher, the one educational resource that will always be in short supply.

Today's educational tasks do not, in the main, require genius, but they may require heroes. Some room for talent, if not genius, remains. To bring the truths of modern science, economics, politics, and psychology to the masses without simplistic distortion will take some doing. Nevertheless, the sincere desire to do this remains a scarcer commodity than the ability. There are good reasons why desire great enough to lead to action, should not be in plentiful supply. Those who seriously undertake to bring truth to others who, because of their large numbers, are most capable of bringing fundamental change—such people run a considerable risk. The Gandhis and Martin Luther Kings do not die in bed. Ché Guevara took weapons into the jungle and followers who could protect themselves and him. He was, beyond doubt, a hero and a martyr. Those who go armed only with the truth will be still more dangerous and also more vulnerable. No one, while he himself remains safe, can in conscience call for heroes. But the heroes have always appeared and—when the time is ripe— will again.

12. STRATEGY FOR A PEACEFUL REVOLUTION

Whereas it appeareth that however certain forms of government are better calculated than others to protect individuals in the free exercise of their natural rights, and are at the same time themselves better guarded against degeneracy, yet experience hath shown, that even under the best forms, those entrusted with power have, in time, and by slow operations, perverted it into tyranny; and it is believed that the most effectual means of preventing this would be, to illuminate, as far as practicable, the minds of the people at large, and more especially to give them knowledge of those facts which history exhibiteth, that, possessed thereby of the experience of other ages and countries, they may be enabled to know ambition under all its shapes, and prompt to exert their natural powers to defeat its purposes.

> Thomas Jefferson
> *"A Bill for the More General Diffusion of Knowledge"*

Strategy for the replacement of schools with universal access to educational resources involves the formulation of specific demands, a statement of the broad goals that justify these demands, and a general plan of action for getting these demands accepted and the goals achieved.

Demands for the just application of existing laws are more easily pressed than legislative programs, and should be used as an entering wedge. In some parts of the United States the federal poverty program has given poor people access to the courts, and they have not been slow to take advantage. Welfare rights, tenant rights, and other civil rights have been won for an increasing number of clients by lawyers paid by the state. Some kinds of action toward deschooling already have a long history, especially legal objections to compulsory schooling by dissident religious sects. More recently, such objections have been based upon non-religious grounds, including the claim that children are not receiving the education that schools purport to give. Suits claiming an equal share of public resources earmarked for education have also been filed, based on the promise of equal protection of the laws contained in the fourteenth amendment. Recently the Supreme Court of the United States has denied the right of employers to impose educational requirements upon candidates for promotion unless they can be shown to be specifically job-related.[1]

We need legislation that would parallel the first amendment to the Constitution of the United States, prohibiting any law with respect to an "establishment of religion." Institutional monopoly of education, especially by the state, has all the evils of a state church, compounded by the fact that a secular school system is sometimes claimed to be neutral with respect to basic values. Since such a claim is obvious nonsense, the defense of a national school system falls back upon the overriding needs and prerogatives of the state. But this involves a contradiction with democratic theory, which holds the state to be the instrument and not the molder of its citizens. The school, in modern times, has become more powerful than the church of the middle ages. The career and, therefore, the life of the individual depend upon his success in school. The law makes him a criminal if he does not attend it. He is subject to its influence far more than medieval man was ever subject to the church. The case for a prohibition of educational monopoly is stronger than the case against a state church, which in times of crisis could oppose the state and claim heavenly authority for its position. The comparable claim to academic freedom is relatively feeble. Churches on the wane did infinitely better against the Nazis and Fascists than universities in the fullness of their power. The school is an instrument of the state and creates subservience to it.

Along with prohibition of an established school, we need an extension of anti-discrimination laws to include schooling. We must forbid favoritism based on schooling as well as on race or religion, and for the same reasons. Where and how one has been schooled is as irrelevant to one's capacity to do a job as race or religion. All affect aspects of job performance that are of interest to the employer but that the law has decided, in the cases of race and religion, are not his legitimate concern. Neither is the school the job applicant went to, or whether he went to school at all, if he can demonstrate the ability to do the job. We are so used to schools that this statement appears strange, yet the logic is simple. We now reserve the best-paid jobs for those whose training has cost the most. If schooling were privately financed, this might be superficially justified in ethical terms, but its economics would still be ridiculous. The public has indeed been schooled to believe that a more-expensive item must be better, but economists explain this on the assumption of price competition among suppliers. Schools have precisely the opposite kind of competition. Even Harvard would be suspect if it were cheap.

In order to equalize educational opportunity, we would have to distribute educational resources in an inverse ratio to present privilege. The argument against such a policy is that it would spend the most money on those with the least aptitude and would produce the least total education. This argument can be challenged, since aptitude judgments are based on success in a school system that discriminates against the poor, but in the end such arguments will not decide a political issue. Many people believe that public resources are equally shared, and if not that they ought to be. A law requiring equal sharing of public educational resources is thus a third item in a legislative program. A system of individual educational accounts would be the only feasible way to enforce such a law.

These three laws would effectively disestablish the school system as an educational monopoly. They would not, however, prevent the development of a new one. By creating an educational market, they would open the way to already powerful economic institutions that might easily take advantage of their power to establish a new monopoly of educational resources.

Effective extension of anti-monopoly laws to the field of education, and effective enforcement of anti-monopoly laws in general, would therefore be a necessary fourth demand. Since such laws are now relatively ineffective in other fields, this demand is far from routine.

Political demands that, if accepted, would result in revolutionary social changes, are formulated not with an expectation of immediate acceptance but for the purpose of creating a revolutionary situation. A demand for the effective enforcement of anti-monopoly laws illustrates this better than the demand for the prohibition of the school monopoly. The latter demand might conceivably be accepted, somewhere, without immediate revolutionary consequences, since it is not schools as such, but a monopoly of enlightenment about the relevant facts of privilege and power that permits privilege and power to continue to be monopolized. But this is the actual issue. The political evil of schools is that they make educational opportunity available only in rough proportion to existing privilege, while conveying the belief that this is not the case.

Commitment to revolutionary change cannot be based entirely upon the recognition of existing evils. A belief that change would be for the better is also necessary. While alternatives to schools have been fairly well spelled out, the broader outlines of a future society in which these alternatives would have to be realized have been only sketchily suggested. Not too much more can be done in the context of a book on education, but the following paragraphs indicate very briefly the premises on which my utopia is predicated.

Defining freedom, in its clearest if not its most complete sense, as freedom *from* rather than freedom *for*, leads to a definition of basic values and factual propositions in largely negative terms. The question becomes, as Paul Goodman says, not what shall we do but what will we tolerate.[2] Philosophies that state in positive terms what is and what should be, seem to lead to the constraint of one human being by another, to the imposition of enlightenment upon the heathen. A philosophy based on the right of maximum freedom from human constraint begins by denying the right of any man to impose either truth or virtue upon another.

The implications of such a philosophy of freedom are very far-reaching. They include, for example, denial of the right to monopolize anything that other men need, since such monopoly is and always has been used to constrain their freedom. Needs, moreover, cannot be restrictively defined as those things immediately needed to sustain life. Denial of information, for example, leads to denial of fresh air, pure water, and nutritious food.

A social and educational philosophy based upon proscription rather than positive values may appear to contradict both the Christian and the liberal traditions. Both, I believe, have been perverted. Jesus said, "I came to fulfill the law," and the Mosaic law, in so far as it applied to human affairs, was written in terms of "thou shalt not." What Jesus taught was simply that fallible human beings can fulfill the law only by going all the way, with others. Because this is uncomfortable doctrine, being your brother's keeper has been swung all the way around from going all the way with him to constraining him—for his own good—to your way; or to God's way, as you interpret it. Liberalism has been even more blatantly perverted. It began as a doctrine of freedom from constraint by others. It has become the forced feeding of persons who have been fenced away from food. Today's welfare programs are obvious attempts to find cheap substitutes for simple justice. We give back to the poor only a fraction of what we take away from them in monopolistic practices, many of which are actual violations of unenforced laws.[3]

Negatively defined freedom is not opposed, as it may superficially appear to be, to a richly positive realization of the good life. It is opposed only to forcing any one concept of such a life upon those who do not share it. Actually, negatively defined freedom provides the only universal basis for positive co-operation. There is no other way of guaranteeing to each human being the opportunity to join with others in any kind of co-operation that does not deny equal opportunities to others.

A world that is to be made by people and not for them cannot be inherited. This rules out political revolution as a means of achieving such a world, since political revolution implies a seizure of concentrated power. Power has often been seized on the pretext that it would be distributed, but it never has been. In progress toward a free, just world, power cannot be seized; it must be destroyed, or rather dissipated, since destruction implies violence, which in turn invites retaliation. A world totally without power is of course impossible, but power can be greatly decentralized, with any necessary concentrations carefully controlled.

Theories of political revolution provide some basis for a more-general theory of institutional revolution, but important revisions and additions are needed. Political institutions are unique among others in the priority they give to the use of violence. In political matters, ideology and rationality tend to be subservient to power and violence. In the case of other institutions—even including the religious—ideology and rationality are relatively more important. This may not always be apparent in the declining days of decadent institutions bolstered by naked power. It is nevertheless true that people choose their markets, their schools, their hospitals, and their transport somewhat less blindly, somewhat more in consideration of costs and benefits—including sentimental attachments—than they choose and defend their citizenship. Changes in non-political institutions are, at least on the surface, subject to rational discussion. Major changes in non-political institutions are at times carried through without violence, although this might be less the case if so-called legitimate violence were not a monopoly of political institutions. It is conceivable, at any rate, that revolutionary change in non-political institutions could take place without violence, could be semirational, and could be affected by analysis, research, and debate. Socialization in the Scandinavian countries and Britain and the formation of the European Common Market provide examples of changes that have taken place in relative peace, though certainly not without pressure and the threat of violence.

Scientific and religious revolutions are worth looking at for ideas. In mature sciences, one major theory controls research and teaching in the field until gradually its deficiencies become more and more widely recognized, it fails to satisfy an increasing set of requirements made upon it, and it is finally discarded in favor of a more successful rival. The necessary conditions for this kind of peaceful change are easy to identify. There is a common language that members of a branch of science use and jointly understand. There is regular communication among scientists. There is an ultimate court of appeal, namely empirical evidence produced under controlled and published conditions. Finally, there are agreed-upon canons of reason and logic. These conditions are hard to match outside the mature sciences, but they provide useful standards, which have actually been approximated in the examples of peaceful institutional change cited above. Thomas Kuhn's recent book and the controversy it has engendered show that even scientific revolutions are vastly idealized in the above account.[4] They do proceed without major violence, however, and with an apparent rationality, at least after the fact.

Religious revolutions have not so commonly been peaceful, but some have been: the spread of Buddhism, for example, of Theosophy, and of more-militant faiths in certain parts of the world. New religious faiths have swept over large areas at a rapid rate, and the conditions under which this has happened have something in common, both with each other and with the conditions under which scientific revolutions have occurred. Sweeping religious changes have always occurred among miserable people, under deteriorating social conditions leading to disillusionment and despair. The other condition for their occurrence has been a powerful and attractive new revelation of truth. Sometimes, but not always, charismatic leaders and disciples have proclaimed the new truth. As in the case of science, common language or translation, communication, and commonly accepted standards of reason and logic are necessary conditions for a religious revolution. The logical standards are not, of course, the same as those of science, and the ultimate test of truth is different. Not evidence for the senses but evidence for the emotions is the touchstone of religious truth. Deeply felt needs must be satisfied. Nevertheless, the parallels between scientific and religious conversion are much more impressive than the differences. Religious revolutions, too, may hold lessons for a theory of institutional revolution.[5]

The annals of violence itself support the idea that violence need not accompany change. Military history is full of instances of battles that were not fought because one side had a demonstrable preponderance of power. Usually this was the side that began with the most power, but not always. A peaceful revolution is not one in which the holders of power give up meekly. This is truly romantic nonsense. A peaceful revolution is one in which the nominal holders of power discover that they have lost their power before they begin to fight.

There is no assurance that institutional revolution can be peaceful. There is only a hope, and not necessarily a very good one. The peaceful character of revolution is not, however, the only consideration. It is important partly because of its critical relation to an even more important criterion. This is that revolution be effective, that it achieve its purposes. The history of political revolution is a history of betrayal, both of the idealists who helped create the conditions for it, and even more of the common people on whose behalf it was made and who themselves made the major sacrifices. Revolution will result in only those positive changes that are in the course of being made when the revolution occurs. If it consists in nothing but these changes, so much the better.

13. WHAT EACH OF US CAN DO

*One makes the revolution
because it is the best way to live.*

Danny the Red

Most of us are not cut out to be heroes, but heroes will be of no avail unless we support them. What we can all do, and must do if there is ever to be a just world, is to begin to live as we would have to live in such a world. If this sounds as if it has been said before—it has. Every great religious leader has said it in one form or another. This makes it neither untrue nor irrelevant, but it is, on the other hand, the best evidence of both its relevance and its truth. If it promises no new magic, guarantees no ultimate victory, but claims only to put humanity back on the main path out of the past, this also is evidence of its truth and relevance.

Power and security, whether based on magic, religion, or science, have always been false beacons leading to the repeated shattering of human hopes. They are false because the attainment of either ultimate power or security would be the final end of everything worth while in human life. People have repeatedly pursued these goals—the prophets of Israel called it idolatry—but people have also, again and again, recognized their idols and turned away from them.

Our modern idols are science and technology, and their temples are the institutions that propagate their worship, and profit from the proceeds. The promise of this modern cult—every man a king, with his private palace and his royal chariot—has captured the fancy of most of mankind. Suppose, even, that it were realized. What would there be to do? Only an endless exchange of royal visits, comparing the quantity and quality of royal plumbing, and an endless drag race of royal chariots, starting from countless crossroads. Eliminate the crossroads, with over- and underpasses, and the whole point of the game would be lost. It would be like checkers with the red and the black playing on separate boards.

But this dream of universal royalty is a pipe dream—only a few can win. Does that make the game worth playing? Not for those who lose. And for those who win? Already they are establishing private arsenals in their suburban redoubts and servicing their Cadillacs with bottled air while they drive through valleys of smog that grow longer and wider and deeper by the day.

So what can people do? They can begin to live as they would have to live in a sane, just world. They can begin again to guard their health, avoiding poisonous air, water, and food and the overeating and underexercise that more than defeat the miracles of modern medicine. There are other millions, of course, who undereat and overexercise because they are forced to work so hard in order to eat at all. What can they do? They can do different things, depending on whether they have the co-operation of the affluent or not. In either case it comes to a matter of sharing—but sharing can be either mutual or unilateral.

People can either increase or decrease their consumption and production, depending on whether they are now doing more or less than their share of the world's work and using more or less than their share of the world's goods. They can share their possessions or their needs. They can conserve, among other things, the natural environment they live in.

Lowering consumption, sharing, and conserving are three actions most of us can take, and yet, jointly, they constitute a powerful revolutionary program. Consider the consequences if this program were consistently practiced in Europe and North America only by those who believe in its principles.

There would be an immediate sharp drop in demand, especially for the more elaborate goods and services. Ever since World War II, production in the North Atlantic community has been directed more and more to the sale of luxury goods, including food, clothing, shelter, and transport for those already fed, clothed, sheltered, and transported much better than most. No small part of the problem of the American economy today is the failure of young people from the upper middle class to establish themselves in the style their parents would gladly support. If only those who share the basic values and beliefs of these young people would follow their example, the market for automobiles, housing, and appliances would collapse. The resulting unemployment would involuntarily curtail the consumption of other people, who would then come to see on what a false foundation their pseudo prosperity had been built. For these people, sharing and conservation would at first be forced consequences of involuntary unemployment, but once—or once more—experienced, they would begin to recommend themselves on their own merits.

Sharing and conservation, applied especially to goods that are supposedly durable, would vastly multiply the economic effect of a mere curtailment of excess consumption. Conserved and shared, there is enough clothing, shelter, and transport in the North Atlantic community to last for a decade. Much of it would need repair and improvement, but this could be supplied without generating much demand even for new raw materials.

Exchange of services, rather than their purchase, whether voluntary or forced, would further deflate the market for goods, services, raw materials, and land. The gross national product of the United States could be cut in half without any reduction in the supply of goods and services that actually benefit anyone. What would happen to the foreign commitments of the United States under these circumstances is another matter, but most of the people of the world would be better off if these commitments were curtailed. What now looks like a scarcity of real resources in much of the world would turn out to be an ample supply, with only the problem of rational use and distribution remaining to be solved. Once faced directly, stripped of its deliberately obscuring façade, this problem, too, might be rationally attacked.

This last statement makes more sense if we remember the political psychology of the great depression. During the thirties, masses of people became aware of the contradictions involved in some people owning and controlling what they could not use and other people needed. Only the fascist movements saved Europe from the consequences of this insight, and only the war saved America. Would fascism occur again if conspicuous consumption broke down for a second time?

The fear and even the covert threat of this prospect keeps many otherwise constructive people immobilized. But only those who do not learn from history are fated to repeat it, and learning does not mean that because one opportunity is missed all others must be forgone.

This is not intended to minimize the dangers that a breakdown of the present system, absurd as it has become, would necessarily entail. These dangers are great, and any way of minimizing them should certainly be grasped. They cannot be avoided, however, by pretending that they result merely from calling attention to the need for basic change or by pretending that the only change needed is to improve the operation of our current institutions. These institutions are basically unsound. They are designed not to meet people's needs but to keep people under control. It would have been safer to change them in the 1930s, before we had the atom bomb. It is safer to change them now than to wait until still more esoteric weapons are invented. The risks of change are great, but the risks of delay are greater.

What, it may be asked, is to prevent the defenders of the status quo from again using totalitarian nationalist parties, international provocation, and war as the means of preserving or re-establishing the present order? Certainly nothing will prevent them from trying. Only enough people deeply committed to a world of sanity and justice, co-operating wisely in their efforts to achieve such a world, would have any chance against those who will assuredly use all means to perpetuate their power and their privilege. But the power of elites declines rapidly when they are forced to rely on violence. They lose the support of even those of their fellows who enjoy their privilege but are unwilling to purchase it once they become aware of its true price. There is no doubt that those who fight for justice, even passively, will pay a price in heightened suffering if privilege is challenged. But the history of Europe during the latest great war provides many examples of how people can protect each other even in the face of overwhelming power ruthlessly applied.

No one can know in advance how, in his own case, the

battle will be joined. In some places, mere withdrawal from excessive consumption and peaceful sharing and conservation in co-operation with like-minded people will produce a majority capable of taking power by legal political means. In other places, civil disobedience as practiced by Gandhi and Nehru in India and by Martin Luther King and his followers in the United States may be necessary. In still other places, the guerrilla tactics that characterized the resistance in Nazi-dominated Europe from 1940–45 may be forced upon people who refuse to continue to support injustice. Strategy and tactics at the three levels of democratic politics, passive resistance, and guerrilla warfare have some important things in common. They all depend upon co-operation rather than coercion. They depend upon local, as opposed to central, leadership. They depend upon a relatively equal sharing of burdens, responsibilities, and rewards. But these are also characteristics of a sane, just world. This is how a worthwhile, viable world will have to be run. People will therefore learn how to run it in the course of bringing it about.

There is probably no other way of creating a society that is of, by, and for the people than through personal co-operation in which each person first orders his own life in the light of shared principles, and then co-operates with others who share these principles. This is how all communities that have enjoyed a reasonable period of sanity and justice have been established—the early United States, Costa Rica, and Uruguay, the ancient Greek and Roman republics, to name only those I know something about.

The Soviet state and the first French republic, established on even nobler principles, but by the replacement of one central power with another, were never able to enjoy the fruits of the sacrifice entailed by their revolutions. Their struggles for power engendered, predominantly, new struggles for power. No sooner, even in the case of communities originally founded on voluntary co-operation, were power and responsibility concentrated than the downfall of these communities began.

What individuals must do, then, is not merely to curtail

consumption, share, and conserve. They must also learn how a just world is organized and governed. For while a great deal is known about past attempts, none of these attempts succeeded, and thus, evidently, not enough was known by those who made them. They were all helped to fail by power seekers, who did their successful best to corrupt them, but they were also helped to fail by the neglect, overconfidence, laziness, interest in other matters, and perhaps most of all, by the ignorance of their members. Brutus and Cassius understood the danger that Caesar represented, but they were too few. Jefferson understood and tried to share his understanding by universalizing education, but was betrayed, unwittingly perhaps, by Horace Mann and other inheritors of the public schools he pioneered.

Perhaps the most important single thing that individuals can do is to take back their responsibility for the education of their children. Children learn very young how power is used by the strong in their relations with the weak, and it is at least possible that this early learning shapes the individual's behavior in all his subsequent relations with those who are stronger or weaker than he.

There is so much that each of us can do to create a just world that the problem is not one of elaborating the ways, but rather one of defining principles of selection. One thing that all ways have in common is some kind of sacrifice. The affluent must enjoy less than they could enjoy. The poor must demand more than they can safely demand. Everyone must learn ways of living and perceiving that are new to him, must risk his own security to help his neighbor in trouble. Affluent parents will have to deny an automobile for each teen-age son and daughter. Poor parents will have to vent their frustrations elsewhere than upon their children. Both will have to allow their children to take risks from which they could protect them.

A strategy of sacrifice must necessarily be selective. People can consistently sacrifice only those things for which the reward exceeds the sacrifice. Especially is this true, since the strategy of sacrifice here described is as necessary after the revolution as during the heat of the battle. A just society cannot first be won and then enjoyed. It must be won anew every day, and must therefore be enjoyed while it is being won.

For sacrifice is not opposed to enjoyment but is its proper alter ego. Health, strength, love, and respect, for example, can be enjoyed only while being earned—or for the briefest time thereafter. Even wealth and power are easily squandered.

Each individual, then, must choose the kind and degree of sacrifice that he can sustain, that for him is rewarding. Some must even be allowed to sacrifice their earned share in a sane, just world. Most people, when they come to understand what is at stake, will not find it so difficult to choose a burden they can bear with pleasure—a discipline they can enjoy. What follows is not intended to restrict, but to amplify, these choices.

One form of sacrifice that many people find rewarding is to trade quantity for quality. When, as frequently happens, this entails choosing the products of artisanry over manufactured goods, the revolutionary consequences in an industrial society may be very great. There is no doubt that manufactured goods are cheaper, in most instances, so that more can be enjoyed for a given amount of money. But one original painting may give more satisfaction than a dozen prints, and this can be true even though the painter is a member of the family. The principle holds for food, clothing, furniture, home construction, and the assembly of jalopies from junk-yard parts. Among the affluent, hobbies can generate demand for tools and new materials more expensive than the finished products. They do not have to, however, nor need art be left to hobbies. It can be a way of life for entire communities, and could be used to advantage by and for the poor on a scale not yet imagined.

The average American household above the poverty line, contains not less than a thousand dollars' worth of unused durable goods, which with a little work, could be made more useful and attractive than goods the poor can afford to buy new at the prices they have to pay. This represents a potential capital of four thousand dollars for each poor American household, the transfer of which would benefit the donors (they could use the space), the poor, and the entrepreneurs who effect the transfer. These entrepreneurs would probably have to have a social rather than an economic motivation, or else a very good façade. Too crass an approach might foul the wellsprings of "charity." Nevertheless, the use of the term entrepreneur is not mere allegory. There would not only have to be middlemen to effect the transfer in question, but thousands of them might come from the ranks of neighborhood businessmen who cannot compete, in the sale of new goods, with nationally organized chains.

In addition to its stock of unused goods, the better-off American household has several thousand dollars' worth of unused space, above what is usually needed for its part-time members and occasional guests. If this excess space were fully utilized, the poor could be as well housed as the affluent. Complete utilization may be hard to imagine, but there are many ways in which a substantial part of this space could be salvaged, which would benefit everyone except real-estate speculators and snobs. Much of this idle space is owned by older people whose families are grown and gone and who cannot sell because the families who could buy do not meet the ethnic requirements of their neighbors. This problem could be overcome by enough acceptable people willing to buy houses as agents for those who suffer discrimination. Another large block of housing space is immobilized because people are afraid to rent rooms or apartments to tenants they feel might expose them to unpleasantness or even danger. This problem could also be overcome by a proper matching of homeowners and tenants.

The two tactics suggested in the paragraph above are opposed in the sense that the first is based on deceit, while the second is based upon restoring trust. This does not make them incompatible. If both were used successfully in the same neighborhood, each would result in the more complete use, and therefore in the greater value, of the neighborhood. Nor are the two tactics politically incompatible. Most people understand the distinction that a man's home is his castle, in which he should be able to choose his associates, while his neighbor's home is not. Nor are the two tactics morally incompatible. It is not that the end justifies the means, but rather that the means chosen in each case appear to be the best available. If this is not actually the case, the suggestions are invalid.

This principle for the selection of means has a broad range of application. Even the law against murder recognizes the right to kill in self-defense or in the defense of others. There are few judicial systems any more that would convict a Jean Valjean for stealing bread to avoid starvation. New laws, on the other hand, complicate current choices. Should people send their children to schools that actually harm them even though the law requires that they do so? Should not people help those who are suffering political persecution even though the law has labeled them criminal? Neither the law nor the prevailing moral code provides a fully dependable criterion for action. In Nazi Germany, both law and current morality required people to collaborate in the murder of their Jewish neighbors. When such major issues as power and privilege are at stake, both laws and mores are used as weapons.

Nevertheless, neither private morality nor the slogan of political revolution—that the ends justify the means—will do. Choosing the best available means is not itself a foolproof formula. But there may often be no other way of choosing courses of action than to apply relevant economic, political, strategic, legal, or moral criteria to the available choices. If the criteria are chosen and applied as others agree they would be applied in the sane, just world that is the goal of action, there may be no better guide.

A third principle is implicit in the above idea of the best available means, namely, the principle of co-operation. It is essential for people to choose and to act as individuals, since only the true consent of individuals can validate the concept of justice. Nevertheless, purely individual action is ineffective and hard to sustain. Individuals must find ways of acting together, but they must personally choose these ways rather than be coerced by superior power. Leadership there can and probably must be, but the leaders rather than the followers should be drafted, and should follow the policies of those they lead.

Co-operation that results in community, physical or functional, has especially great advantages. The future world must be based on community and, throughout most of the modern world, community has been lost. Even the traditional communities that remain may have to be re-created, since it is doubtful that people given a real choice will settle for the drudgery and hierarchy that characterize most traditional communities. But there are also important strategic advantages in community effort. Communities can often legitimately take over much of the lawmaking and police power. They can also serve as examples of sanity and justice to the outside world.

In all the above there is, obviously, nothing new. Even what may seem original is merely a new dress on an old-fashioned idea. We have become used to thinking of reality in terms of pentagons and atom bombs or, before that, in terms of armies, navies, banks, and corporations. People's movements are thought to belong to the dark ages. Yet the oldest part of the United States is less than two hundred years old; the independent nations of South America have scarcely more than a century of history, while those of Africa and Asia, including Israel, were founded by popular movements only a few decades ago. The Viet Cong, among others, seem to have a pretty good thing going right now.

It is true that, up to now, military action has often been decisive, but the present rulers of China won their battles with weapons captured from the enemy, while in India there was no military showdown at all.

Three things are new that lend substance to what used to be, and still is, called, utopian dreaming. First, drudgery is out of date. Second, modern institutions require increasingly universal co-operation. Third, universal education is now possible. It was only yesterday that the labor of four people was required to feed five. England had to fence people off the land in order to fill her factories. Today most people are in the way, both in the factory and in the field. Food and all other physical products can be produced more efficiently without them. People are indispensable, however, as passive clients and supporters of the production complex—taking what they are offered and doing what they are told. Without their co-operation, the current system for control of production and distribution would collapse. Increasingly, people are becoming aware of these facts—realizing that their bodies are no longer required for mass production and that they are being asked instead to surrender their judgment and their will to its dictates.

But to whose dictates? Production is a mindless thing. It knows no imperatives as to what shall be produced, where, when, and for whom. The invisible hand is somebody's hand behind the curtain. More and more people are beginning to realize that they should be deciding these things, along with others, and that actually everyone has an equal right to decide them. When everyone understands this, universal education will be well on its way. There will still be a lot to learn: how to do one's share, how to claim one's share and no more, how to co-operate with others in things that cannot be done alone. These lessons will never be completely learned, but when everyone has a reasonable opportunity to learn and to apply them, things will begin to move.

All this, if it were mere exhortation, would still be whistling in the dark. But things are happening. Charles Reich, in *The Greening of America*, says that a people's revolution has begun. Young people all over the world are tuning out the system and turning themselves on. Older people, including many who are concerned by the tactics of the young, still share their sense of the absurdity of the world they live in. The deprived, especially those who live in the prosperous countries, are opening their eyes and flexing their muscles. The great masses of the deprived, in Africa, Asia, and South America, are still largely quiescent. When they begin to stir, the thunder may at first roll softly, but it will be heard. We can turn it on.

NOTES AND REFERENCES

Foreword

1. In 1961 Ivan Illich, Feodora Stancioff, and Brother Gerry Morris founded CIDOC, originally called the Center of Intercultural Formation, in Cuernavaca. During its first six years, the center was devoted mainly to educational programs for missionaries to Latin America. This period ended at about the time Illich published an article called "The Seamy Side of Charity" in the Jesuit magazine *America,* which called into serious question the very idea of sending North American missionaries to Third World countries. Since 1967, CIDOC (Centro Intercultural de Documentación) has concentrated on the analysis of various modern institutions, especially the school. During this period, CIDOC has hosted the seminar on alternatives in education that I have directed.
2. The current rate of population increase in Costa Rica is three times the current world rate. United Nations, Demographic Statistics, Annual Reports.
3. George Dennison, *The Lives of Children: The Story of First Street School* (New York: Random House, 1969).
4. Jonathan Kozol, *Death at an Early Age* (New York: Bantam Books, Inc., 1968).
5. Floyd H. Allport, *Institutional Behavior* (Chapel Hill, N.C.: Chapel Hill Press, 1933).

Chapter 1

1. Enrollment figures by grade, compiled by UNESCO, show that only in a minority of even those more advanced countries that have such data do more than a small fraction of the students enrolled in the first grade complete elementary school. UNESCO, Enrollment Data, Annual Reports, Paris.

2. For a further development of the "ladder" image of society, see the concluding chapter in Raymond Williams, *Culture and Society, 1780–1950* (Harmondsworth, Middlesex: Penguin Books, Ltd., 1958).

3. *La instrucción pública en Puerto Rico, ayer, hoy y mañana*, Department of Public Instruction, Commonwealth of Puerto Rico, 1968.

4. *Ibid*.

5. Monographs, International Institute for Educational Planning, Paris.

6. From data compiled by the Organization for Economic and Cultural Development for member countries. OECD, Paris. See, for example, Background Study No. 1, for the Conference on Policies for Educational Growth.

7. This estimate is based on two studies commissioned by the United States Office of Education in 1969. Two groups of educators, working independently, were asked to set forth the currently unmet needs in American elementary and high school education. The costs of meeting these needs were then calculated in terms of current unit costs as published in the USOE annual report. The independent estimates were within a few billion dollars of each other. These studies have not been published. Their results were made available by Kenneth Parsley, Director of the Office of Organization and Methods of the USOE, Department of Health, Education and Welfare, Washington, D.C.

8. National accounts data, United States and other countries. Published annually by the United Nations.

9. In comparing the cost of education in school and on the job, all school costs are attributed to the education that occurs in school, while only training time on the job is charged to the education that occurs at work. Our analysis of the functions of schooling might appear to invalidate such an attribution, and for other purposes it would. For this specific purpose, of comparing educational costs in school and at work, it seems justified. The money the public pays for production is paid for the products of work. The money paid for schooling, as far as the public is concerned, goes for education. In neither case does the public get what it pays for, but in comparing costs it must be assumed that it does.

10. These calculations were made by the author, based on school cost data from the annual reports of the U. S. Office of Education, supplemented by information contained in such special reports as the Coleman study on equal opportunity. There are no official data on enrollment by family income nor on expenditure by family income, but there are many bases for estimate and for cross-checking the validity of estimates. I believe that I have been in all instances

conservative, and invite others to make independent estimates and to check my calculations.

11. Based on an Evaluative Report on Title I entitled "Education of the Disadvantaged," published by the U. S. Office of Education, fiscal year 1968. This report found, among other things, that less than one dollar of every three allocated to Title I projects, which were supposed to supplement the education of children whose families had incomes below $3000 per year, was actually spent on these children. The rest was spent on other children of higher family income enrolled in the same school system or on general support of the system.

12. These calculations were made by Ivan Illich, based on official enrollment and expenditure data supplied by the Bolivian government. They were reported to a specially constituted policy board of the Bolivian government, by Illich personally, and were accepted as valid. They reflect primarily the fact that only a tiny percentage of the population survives the early elementary grades, and that all the cost of secondary and higher education must be attributed to this tiny minority.

13. Based on compilations prepared by the U. S. Office of Education, which in turn are based on financial data reported by the various states, and published annually by USOE.

14. Frederick Harbison and C. A. Myers, *Manpower and Education: Country Studies in Economic Development* (New York: McGraw-Hill, 1965).

15. Analysis of demographic data in many developing countries shows that the number of children born to women during their total childbearing period declines markedly for women with more than four to six years of schooling, especially in urban areas. A detailed study of declining birth rates in Japan shows that while schooling and urban residence are both related statistically to lower birth rates, the most critical factor is a shift in the vocational basis of family support from traditional rural to modern urban occupations. Irene Taeuber, *Population of Japan* (Princeton, N.J.: Princeton University Press, 1958).

16. From data compiled by the Economic Commission for Latin America, Santiago de Chile.

17. Richard Hoggart brilliantly describes the psychological effects of schooling on scholarship students recruited from England's working class in *The Uses of Literacy* (Oxford: Oxford University Press, 1957).

18. John Holt, *How Children Fail* (New York: Dell Publishing Co., 1964).

Chapter 2

1. Unpublished study of pupil/teacher relations using ethnographic (participant-observer) methods. Anthony Lauria, Planning Department, Puerto Rico Department of Instructions, 1968.

2. In this light see the history of labor opposition to high schools, in Merle E. Curti, *The Social Ideas of American Educators* (Patterson, N.J.: Littlefield, Adams & Co., 1959).

3. R. Gurjoy, unpublished paper read at the Conference on Development Planning, sponsored by the Public Administration Department of the State University of New York, held at Saratoga Springs, November 11–24, 1969. For similar evidence see the various books of R. D. Laing.

4. Paul Bady, "L'enseignement en Chine," *Esprit*, 37e année 399, Janvier 1971, pp. 73–88.

5. Michael Young, *The Rise of the Meritocracy* (New York: Pelican Paperbacks, Penguin Press, 1970).

6. John Kenneth Galbraith, *The New Industrial State* (New York: The New American Library, Inc., 1967).

7. Arthur R. Jensen, "How Much Can We Boost IQ and Scholastic Achievement?" *Harvard Educational Review* (Winter 1969).

8. A. S. Neill's Summerhill and schools patterned after it may be partial exceptions.

9. W. Dennis and P. Najarian, "Infant Development Under Environmental Handicap," *Psychological Monographs* 71:7.

10. The failures of ghetto schools in the United States are detailed in more documents than can be listed. Among them are:

    Report on Equality of Opportunity in Education, U. S. Department of Health, Education and Welfare (U. S. Government Printing Office, Washington, D.C., 1966).

    Herbert Kohl, *36 Children* (New York: The New American Library, 1968).

    Jonathan Kozol, *Death at an Early Age* (New York: Bantam Books, Inc., 1968).

11. The failures of Brazilian rural schools are best illustrated in the dropout figures. More than half drop out before the beginning of the third grade, and according to many studies conducted by UNESCO among other organizations, dropouts at this level have not achieved functional literacy.

12. Paulo Freire and Paul Goodman, two current philosophers of education proceeding from quite different premises, both provide carefully reasoned support for this point of view. Paulo Freire is a Brazilian educator known for his success in teaching peasants to read and write effectively with a minimum investment of time and

facilities. A gross oversimplification of his position is that people learn only in the process of becoming conscious of their true-life situation—coming to see this situation clearly under circumstances that permit them to act effectively upon it. Schools could never provide their students with the action potential that this program requires. It is interesting that Dewey called for something like this action potential in his proposed experimental schools, which never actually came into being.

Goodman's position, in equally oversimplified form, is not easily distinguished from Freire's. Goodman holds that people learn what they need to learn in the course of real-life encounters. Professions and trades are learned by practicing them. Scholars develop in communities of scholars. Schools can teach only alienated knowledge: knowledge divorced from both its origins and its applications, and therefore dead knowledge.

The effect of transmitting dead knowledge, according to Freire, is to domesticate rather than educate. Domestication is training in conformity and the development of either magical or mythical attitudes toward those aspects of life which contradict the pressures toward conformity. According to Goodman the attempt to transmit dead knowledge either has no effect or leads to a sense that the world is absurd. Both men are probably right. The real world of the Brazilian peasant is perhaps too grim to be seen as absurd and must, therefore, be either repressed or enshrouded in magic. The New Yorker, on the other hand, may be protected enough to be able to view the grimness of his world through the semitransparent veil of absurdity.

Paulo Freire, "The Adult Literacy Process as Cultural Action for Freedom," *Harvard Educational Review*, Vol. 40, No. 2, May 2, 1970, pp. 205–25. Also *Pedagogy of the Oppressed* (New York: Herder & Herder, 1970).

Paul Goodman, *Growing Up Absurd* (New York: Alfred A. Knopf, 1960).

Joel Spring, "Education and the Rise of the Corporate State," CIDOC, 1970.

13. The 1910 United States census, which included Puerto Rico for the first time, showed a majority of the adult population to be literate, though fewer than 10% had attended school.

14. The Coleman *Report on Equality of Opportunity in Education*, *supra*, shows that home background, including the education of parents, explains much more of the difference in student achievement than the quality of schools attended by these students as measured in costs, teacher preparation, etc.

15. Analysis of achievement-test scores for all students who took high school algebra in the Puerto Rico public schools in 1964 shows a random distribution of answers on all items except the four

or five easiest, which were essentially simple arithmetic problems. Other student populations may do somewhat better, but both Project Talent, conducted by Flanagan et al. at the University of Pittsburgh, and Torsten Husén's, *Achievement in Mathematics in Twelve Countries* (International Educational Achievement Association Project of the Institute of Pedagogy, Hamburg, Germany) show that differences between school systems and between countries are relatively small. Item analyses are not available for these other populations.

It will be noted that statements of fact in the text are frequently supported with Puerto Rican data. This is partially because the author worked for fifteen years with Puerto Rican school data, but also because very few school systems have data as comprehensive, in as much detail, and so well analyzed. This, again, is because Puerto Rico has one of the largest integrated school systems of the world. In the United States only New York City's is larger. Another reason is that school systems in general are not given to quantitative evaluation. Puerto Rico has limited resources, but from 1946 to 1968 enjoyed a very progressive government. Finally, its school system had a series of outstanding directors of evaluation culminating in the work of Charles O. Hammil, who is responsible for most of the analyses cited.

16. Jerome S. Bruner, Rose R. Olver, Patricia M. Greenfield, et al., *Studies in Cognitive Growth*, A Collaboration at the Center for Cognitive Studies (New York: John Wiley & Sons, Inc., 1967).

Chapter 3

1. Philippe Ariès, *Centuries of Childhood* (New York: Vintage Books, 1962).
2. Torsten Husén, *International Study of Achievement in Mathematics*, 2 vols. (New York: John Wiley & Sons, Inc., 1967).
3. Ivar Berg, *Education and Jobs: The Great Training Robbery* (New York: Praeger Publications, 1970).
4. Richard Hoggart, *Uses of Literacy: Changing Patterns in English Mass Culture* (Oxford: Oxford University Press, 1957).

Chapter 4

1. Joseph M. Hunt, *Intelligence and Experience* (New York: Ronald, 1961).
2. "Another alternative to working class solidarity offered is the idea of individual opportunity—of the ladder. It has been one of the forms of service to provide such a ladder, in industry, in educa-

tion, and elsewhere . . . Yet the ladder is a perfect symbol of the bourgeois idea of society, because while undoubtedly it offers the opportunity to climb, it is a device which can only be used individually: you go up the ladder alone. . . . My own view is that the ladder version of society is objectionable in two related aspects: first, that it weakens the principle of common betterment, which ought to be an absolute value; second, that it sweetens the poison of hierarchy, in particular by offering the hierarchy of merit as a thing different in kind from the hierarchy of money or of birth." Raymond Williams, *Culture and Society, 1780–1950* (Harmondsworth, Middlesex: Penguin Books, Ltd., 1958), pp. 317–18.

3. New knowledge has meaning only in the perspective of the past. Schools were once such champions of this principle that the word scholastic still carries opprobrium in certain circles. Modern schools have done a complete turnabout. They pay lip service to meaning and reserve their obeisance for relevance. Nor can they blame students for this. Having made themselves the gateway to all other secular delights, they cannot wonder that students storm the gates.

Chapter 5

1. Joseph Campbell, *The Masks of God*, 3 vols. (New York: Viking Press, 1969).
2. H. I. Marrou, *A History of Education in Antiquity*, tr. by George Lamb (New York: Mentor Books, 1964).
3. Edward Chiera, *They Wrote on Clay* (Chicago: University of Chicago Press, 1938).
4. Richard L. Nettleship, *The Theory of Education in the Republic of Plato* (New York: Teachers College Press, Columbia University, 1968). See also, Marrou, op. cit., Chapter VI: "The Masters of the Classical Tradition."
5. Aristophanes, *The Clouds*, in *The Plays of Aristophanes*, tr. by Benjamin Bickly Rogers, ed. by William Barton (Chicago: Encyclopaedia Britannica Press, Great Books of the Western World No. 5, 1952). See also, Marrou, op. cit., Chapter IV: "The Old Athenian Education."
6. Marrou, op. cit.
7. David Knowles, *The Monastic Order in England* (Cambridge: The University Press, 1941).
8. M. H. Vicaire, *Histoire de Saint Dominique*, 2 vols. (Paris: Cerf, 1957). W. A. Hinnebusch, *History of the Dominican Order* (New York: Alba, 1966).
9. Kajetan Esser, *Anfange und Ursprungliche Zielsetzungen des Ordens der Minderbruder* (Leiden: E. J. Brill, 1966).

10. H. Outram Evennett, *The Spirit of the Counter-Reformation* (New York: Cambridge University Press, 1969).

James Broderick, *The Origin of the Jesuits* (Garden City, N.Y.: Doubleday & Co., 1960).

11. Paul Goodman, *The Community of Scholars* (New York: Random House Press, 1962).

12. In addition to the invention of printing, the fifteenth century brought on an expansion of commercial activities, which created a demand for a different kind of instruction. "Reading and writing" schools appeared in England and northern Germany. These were opposed by the clergy, and a compromise was reached under which they were allowed to continue, but forbidden to teach Latin, thus preserving the clerical monopoly on elite education. Luther deplored students going to these schools when, with the breakdown of monastic education and the old Church system, studies no longer led to places in the ecclesiastical bureaucracy. In sixteenth-century England the reading and writing schools were establishments in which "letter writing and practical accounting were taught, for a new class" (Raymond Williams, *The Long Revolution, supra,* p. 151).

13. Johann G. Fichte, Addresses to the German Nation (New York: Harper & Row, 1968).

14. Cf. Louis René de Caradeux de la Chalotais, *Essay on National Education* (London: Edward Arnold, 1934).

F. de la Fontainerie, *French Liberalism and Education in the Eighteenth Century. The Writings of La Chalotais, Turgot, Diderot and Condorcet on National Education* (New York: McGraw-Hill, 1932).

15. Cf. Mona Ozouf, *L'École, l'Église et la République, 1871–1914* (Paris: Armand Colin, 1963).

16. Merle E. Curti, *The Social Ideas of American Educators* (Paterson, N.J.: Littlefield, Adams & Co., 1959).

17. Joel H. Spring, "Education as a Form of Social Control," the first of a series of conferences given at CIDOC in February 1970. (Cuernavaca, Mexico: CIDOC Doc. 70/221, 1970).

18. Horace Mann, *The Republic and the School: Horace Mann on the Education of Free Men,* ed. by Lawrence A. Cremin (New York: Teachers College Press, Columbia University, 1957).

19. Thomas Jefferson, *Crusade against Ignorance: Thomas Jefferson on Education,* ed. Gordon C. Lee, New York, Teachers College Press, Columbia University, 1961.

20. Cf. Michael Katz, "From Voluntarism to Bureaucracy in American Education," in *Formative Undercurrents of Compulsory Knowledge,* Cuernavaca, CIDOC, 1970, p. 2/14.

21. John Dewey, *John Dewey on Education: Selected Writings,*

ed. by Reginald D. Archanbault (New York: Random House, 1964).

Chapter 6

1. Mark Arnold Foster, "Poison in the Air," *Manchester Guardian Weekly*, August 15, 1970.
2. Mohandas K. Gandhi, *Autobiography* (New York: Beacon Press, 1957). *The Essential Gandhi*, ed. by Louis Fisher (New York: Vintage Paperbacks, Random House Press, 1962).
3. Janet Reiner, Everett Reimer, and Thomas Reiner, "Client Analysis and the Planning of Public Programs," *Journal of the American Institute of Planners*, Nov. 1963. Bernard J. Frieden and Robert Morris, eds. *Urban Planning and Social Policy* (New York: Basic Books, 1968).
4. Thorstein Veblen, *The Theory of the Leisure Class* (New York: Mentor Books, 1954).
5. This has failed to occur only in areas where development has progressed very rapidly, with correspondingly heavy imports of foreign capital and manpower. Israel, Puerto Rico, and Taiwan—significantly, all very small—are the only unequivocal examples. In these areas, war, migration, and strategic location, respectively, have made it possible to engage the entire population in the development process, thus avoiding the social split and alienation of the non-participating element. These exceptions, therefore, prove the rule—unless it can be shown that all nations would accept similar relationships with the developed world and that comparable rates of foreign investment could be achieved on a world-wide scale.[7]

Japan and the communist nations are special cases. The latter, by taking over the pricing mechanism, were able to force their total populations into their institutions. By doing so, they succeeded in avoiding the dilemmas of the Third World, but the procrustean character of their institutional frameworks and the attendant difficulties are well known. These difficulties resulted, in considerable part, from the wholesale adoption of precommunist institutions, unadapted to the purposes they were supposed to serve. By fiat, these institutions involved the whole population, but not in ways that resulted in high levels of motivation for socially constructive activity.

Japan's ability to maintain the character of her traditional social structure gave her a less costly means than that of the communist states. Employers were responsible for employment security, and employees were willing to accept the wages offered.[8] But Japan also shared the advantages of the nations that pioneered economic development, in that she enjoyed a substantial political and economic empire, which permitted her to export goods, services, and manpower.

What this means for development strategy is that developing nations must invent their own institutions. Obviously these institutions must be able to use foreign components—machinery, materials, techniques, knowledge, even trained manpower. What must be indigenous are the basic institutions that determine who gets what, when, and at what price. They must not only be indigenous, however, but also new. The church and the hacienda will obviously not do, since they originally opened the door to foreign institutions. The feudal plantations of northeast Brazil, for example, originally provided a role, however humble, for the inhabitants of that area.[9] The importation of modern machinery reduced the demand for labor, while the importation of modern drugs increased its supply to the point where the masses of this region are now starving. A return to the hacienda would merely accelerate the current rate of starvation.

What must be new and indigenous are the institutional patterns —which determine how major classes of needs will be satisfied; how people will be fed, clothed, sheltered, educated, and protected from danger, disease, misfortune, and exploitation.[10] Much of the technology of the modern world will be required, but it will have to be applied in a way that meets the needs of the needy.

This is impossible within the framework of the institutions of the developed world. Using the same institutions, the Third World could never catch up. The educationally more-advanced nations must forever remain better educated if schools are to be the means of education. And Brazil, spending fifty dollars per student per year, can never have the schools that in North America cost a thousand dollars. Transportation can never catch up unless the less-developed nation installs more-efficient factories than the developed nation. But seldom can the less-developed nation install a factory even nearly as good. If this is done in a particular case, major and expensive components must be bought from the developed nation at a price that forces this case to be an exception. The follower must, therefore, not only remain behind but fall further behind as long as he adopts the means of development of the leader.

The underdeveloped society requires more-efficient institutions than those of the developed: more food, clothing, shelter, learning, and protection per unit of input than modern agriculture, manufacture, construction, schooling, etc., can supply. This is possible only by departing from different premises. India may never be able to produce the U.S. diet, but only the producers of Coca-Cola, scotch whisky, corn-fed beef, and the doctors and dentists who live on the consumers thereof really benefit from this diet. Better clothing, shelter, education, and protection than the standard products of the North Atlantic community are no more difficult to design than is a superior diet. Neither is there great difficulty in designing better means of producing these goods and services than the ones now in vogue.

6. Gunnar Myrdal, *Rich Lands and Poor* (New York: Harper & Row, 1958).

P. A. Ehrlich, *Population Bomb* (New York, Ballantine Press).

Alfred Sauvy, *Fertility and Survival: Population Problems from Malthus to Mao Tse-Tung* (New York: Collier, 1962).

7. UN Annual Statistics on Rates of Development and Investment from Foreign Sources.

8. James C. Abegglen, *Japanese Factory* (New York: Free Press, 1965).

9. Celso Furtado, *Development and Underdevelopment*, tr. by Ricardo de Aquilar and Eric C. Drysdale (Berkeley: University of California Press, 1963).

———, *Economic Growth of Brazil*, tr. by Ricardo de Aquilar and Eric C. Drysdale (Berkeley: University of California Press, 1963).

Albert O. Hirschman, *Journeys Toward Progress: Studies of Economic Policy Making in Latin America* (New York: The Twentieth Century Fund, 1963).

10. Ivan Illich, "Outwitting the Developed Countries," *The New York Review of Books*, New York, 13(8), November 6, 1969. Also in Illich, *Celebration of Awareness*, Chapter Eleven (New York: Doubleday, 1970).

Chapter 7

1. Alex Bavelas and others have experimented with small groups in which communication is variously channeled. While there is no direct relationship between Bavelas' work and the hypothesis proposed here, there are certain parallels that suggest a possible common theoretical explanation. Alex Bavelas, "Task Oriented Groups," Journal of the American Acoustical Society, 1950; 22, 727–30.

2. John Kenneth Galbraith, *The New Industrial State* (New York: Signet Books, 1967).

3. John Kenneth Galbraith, *The Affluent Society* (Boston, Mass.: Houghton Mifflin, 1958).

4. G. William Skinner, "Marketing and Social Structure in Rural China," from *Peasant Society, A Reader* (Boston, Mass.: Little, Brown and Company, Inc., 1967).

5. It might be argued that electricity, for example, is as addictive as are the household appliances that use it. Judged in terms of withdrawal symptoms, this might appear to be so, but a sharper cri-

terion of addiction is the need for ever more of a product in order to produce the same degree of satisfaction. Here, electricity in the absense of appliances or other devices, does not qualify, while the appliances clearly do. Water works the same way. People do not drink more or wash more except as more clothes, better detergents, or water-wasting washing machines are introduced.

Chapter 8

1. José Ortega y Gasset, *Revolt of the Masses* (New York: Norton, 1932).
2. Jane Jacobs, *The Economy of Cities* (New York: Vintage Books, 1967).

Chapter 9

1. The author observed this experiment in person in 1966, saw the attendants behind each child, and talked to the computer programmers and to the research staff.
2. To persons inclined to dispute this principle of instruction, let me point out that almost all educators pay at least lip service to the idea that the most important thing a student can learn is how to learn. He may be helped to learn how to learn by wise counsel and supervisors, but he will certainly never learn how to learn without making the basic decisions involved in the learning process, nor can he begin to learn this too early in life, which is not to say, however, that total freedom is ever possible or desirable.
3. Walter Bagehot, *Physics and Politics*.
4. Thomas Kuhn, *The Structure of Scientific Revolutions* (Chicago: University of Chicago Press, 1962).

Chapter 10

1. These calculations are based on projected public expenditures for education at all levels for 1971 of $50 billion. They assume an eligible population of 200 million and an average lifetime of sixty-eight years. Projections of Educational Statistics, U. S. Government Printing Office. OE-10030-68.

Chapter 11

1. Paulo Freire, *Cultural Action: A Dialectic Analysis* (published at Cuernavaca, Mexico: CIDOC Cuaderno 1004, 1970).

———, "The Adult Literacy Process as Cultural Action for Freedom," *Harvard Educational Review* 40:2, May 1970, pp. 205–25.
———, "Cultural Action and Conscientization," *Harvard Educational Review* 40:3, August 1970, pp. 452–78.
2. Cf. for example: Jacques Monast, *L'Univers Religieux des Aymaras de Bolivie* (Cuernavaca, Mexico: CIDOC, Sondeos No. 10, 1966).

Chapter 12

1. *Griggs et al.* v. *Duke Power Company:* In this decision the Court forbade the use of scholastic requirements or tests that are not specifically related to the job. The immediate scope of the decision is limited to cases in which racial discrimination is alleged, but the language of the decision is broad and is sure to invite extension to other areas.
2. An oral statement made by Paul Goodman in the course of a seminar held by the International Association for Cultural Freedom at Aspen, Colorado, August 29 to September 3, 1970.
3. Testimony given before a U. S. Senate subcommittee on monopoly headed by Senator Philip Hart of Michigan contains estimates that monopoly pricing accounts for 25% of the gross national product. Almost regardless of how the impact of these prices on the poor is calculated, it comes to more than they receive in welfare and other benefit programs.
4. Thomas S. Kuhn, *The Structure of Scientific Revolutions* (Chicago: The University of Chicago Press, 1962).
5. Norman Cohn, *The Pursuit of the Millennium* (New York: Harper & Row, 1961).

INDEX